THE

BACKWORDS DICTIONARY

THE

BACKWORDS DICTIONARY

A Word Ending Dictionary

EDITED BY
RICHARD EKSTROM

Dedicated to:

Sandra, Rachel, Albert, Virginia, & Esther

With thanks to Bruce Guthrie & William Weil

CONTENTS

INTRODUCTION

This dictionary was written primarily to enhance the enjoyment in playing the game of Scrabble®, although poets, rhymers, players of crossword puzzles and other word games may also find it useful.

In our family, Scrabble is a game we play for our enjoyment and amusement. As such, we are not opposed to modifying the rules to increase our enjoyment. For example, we might modify the number of tiles each player might have. Less experienced players would have more; while more experienced players would have less. This is an especially helpful practice when playing with an exchange student whose English is developing. At other times, if we want a fast game, every player will play with extra tiles, perhaps nine or ten.

And, we enjoy playing with a dictionary. We use a dictionary not because we want to challenge our opponent, but because we want to learn new words, find the perfect fit for a triple word score, reduce frustration when our memories are working slowly, and we've just come to enjoy playing that way.

The design for this dictionary evolved over a period of years. I kept notes on the size of words we typically made, what kind of situations posed difficulties in finding words, and great scoring opportunities missed. There were four major observations.

First, as casual players, we rarely created words in a single turn which were more than five letters long in total, unless it was done with a prefix such as *ex, de, re, pre* or *un,* or a suffix such as *ed, ing, s or y*. At the same time, most dictionaries are filled with lots of words longer than five letters. This causes visual clutter which is not only time consuming, but makes it harder to find words you might be able to actually use. In addition, the probability of being able to make some words is extremely small, for example, *zyzzyva* (a tropical weevil). The odds of having the only z, both *y's*, both *blanks* (for the other two *z's),* and a v is astronomical. This, of course, is an extreme example, and The Backwords Dictionary has its share of improbables, but by limiting the dictionary to words with a maximum of five letters, it is useful for its purpose.

The second observation, and the one for which the dictionary is named, is that about 35-40% of the time, a player wants to create a word ending in a specific letter. This, however, is not the way we traditionally think, and, not to mention, this is not the way dictionaries are sorted. In other words, in many situations, conventional dictionaries are not arranged in an easy to use manner. This dictionary solves that problem by sorting on the last letter of the word. Of course, you will still need a conventional dictionary for the 35-40% of the time you need a word beginning with a specific letter. (The other 20-30% are words where the focus letter is neither the first or the last.)

The third observation is that certain letters present special challenges. These are *J, Q, X,* and Z. These are the highest point value letters and, since there is only one of each, it is natural to want to optimize the opportunity. Hence, each of those letters has a chapter for all the words which have the individual letter, regardless of the position - first, last, or somewhere in the middle.

The fourth observation was that often a significant number of points could be scored with just two or three letters. Typically there were two parts to this observation: taking advantage of a difficult to get at multiple value square and, making two or even three words simultaneously. The key is two letter words. They let you fit into tight spots, and, if you can run a couple of them alongside another word, you will often get a surprising number of points. Knowing two letter words is also very valuable at the end of the game when you want to use up your tiles, but don't want to settle for just two points.

Purists may reject the idea of using a dictionary, but for us it is a lot of fun.

I hope you enjoy the game from this different perspective.

Richard Ekstrom

Pittsburgh, Pennsylvania

SCRABBLE FACTOIDS

Scrabble was invented in 1938 by architect Alfred Mosher Butts.

Scrabble is a real word. It means "to scratch frantically."

Butts decided on the frequency and distribution of letters in Scrabble by analyzing the front page of The New York Times.

The original name of Scrabble was "Criss-Crosswords"

The highest known score for a single word in competition Scrabble is 392 for the word "caziques", which means Indian chief. Other theoretical words to score 392 are oxazepam, beziques, mezquits, mesquite.

The highest possible score a player can get in Scrabble, on a first turn, is for the word "mujiks" (128 points).

The highest possible score, theoretically, for a single play under American tournament Scrabble rules is 1,778 points for joining eight already played tiles to form the word "oxyphenbutazone" across three triple-word score squares, while simultaneously extending seven specific already-played words to form new words.

AA	rough, cindery lava
ABA	sleeveless garment
ABACA	Philippine plant
ABAKA	abaca
ABOMA	South American snake
ABORA	away from the mouth
ACETA	of acetum
ACTA	recording proceedings
AECIA	cuplike structures
AGA	high-ranking Turkish military officer
AGAMA	a tropical lizard
AGHA	aga
AGMA	eng
AGORA	marketplace in ancient Greece
AHA	expression of surprise, triumph, or derision
AJIVA	inanimate matter
AKELA	Cub Scout pack leader
ALA	a wing or wing like part
ALMA	almah – young Hebrew girl
ALOHA	a greeting or farewell
ALPHA	Greek letter
ALULA	tuft of feathers or first digit of a bird's wing
AMA	amah
AMEBA	amoeba
AMIA	a freshwater fish
AMIGA	a female friend
ANA	information about a particular subject
ANGA	any of the eight practices of yoga
ANIMA	the soul
ANNA	a former coin of India
ANOA	a wild ox
ANSA	genus of moth

ANTA	a pilaster formed top of a wall
ANTRA	cavity within a bone
AORTA	a main artery
AQUA	water
AREA	section of the cerebral cortex
ARECA	a tropical tree
ARENA	an enclosed area for contents
ARTA	elaborate melody for a single voice
AROMA	a pleasant odor
ATMA	atman
ATRIA	of atrium
AURA	an invisible emanation
AVA	at all
AWA	away
BA	the eternal soul in Egyptian mythology
BAA	to bleat
BABA	a rum cake
BABKA	a coffee cake
BACCA	a berry
BAIZA	a monetary unit of Oman
BALSA	a tropical tree
BELGA	former Belgian monetary unit
BEMA	platform in a synagogue
BETA	a Greek letter
BETTA	a freshwater fish
BIMA	bema
BIOTA	the flora and fauna of a region
BOA	a large snake
BOHEA	a black tea
BOLA	a throwing weapon
BORA	a cold wind

BOYLA	a witch doctor	CURIA	a court of justice
BRA	a brassiere	CYMA	a curved molding
BRAVA	a shout of approval	DA	used in names
BRAZA	a Spanish unit of length	DACHA	a Russian cottage
BULLA	a large blister	DADA	artistic and literary movement
BUNYA	an evergreen tree		
BURA	buran	DATA	of datum
BURSA	a bodily pouch	DELTA	deposit at mouth of river
BWANA	master; boss	DERMA	a layer of the skin
CALLA	a tropical plant	DEVA	a Hindu god
CANNA	a tropical plant	DICTA	of dictum
CASA	a dwelling	DITA	a Philippine tree
CEIBA	a tropical tree	DIVA	distinguished female operatic singer
CELLA	interior of an ancient temple		
		DOBLA	former gold coin of Spain
CERTA	a chemical compound	DOBRA	a former gold coin of Portugal
CESTA	a basket used in jai alai		
CHELA	a pincer like claw	DOGMA	a principle or belief put forth as authoritative
CHIA	a Mexican herb		
CHINA	fine porcelain ware	DONA	a Spanish lady
CHUFA	a European sedge	DONNA	an Italian lady
CILIA	of cilium	DOPA	an amino acid
CIRCA	around	DORSA	of dorsum
COALA	koala	DOUMA	duma
COBTA	a large game fish	DOURA	durra
COBRA	a venomous snake	DRAMA	a composition written for theatrical performance
COCA	a South American shrub		
COCOA	chocolate	DULIA	veneration given to saints
CODA	a passage at the end of a musical composition	DUMA	a Russian council
		DUMKA	a Slavic folk ballad
COLA	a carbonated beverage	DURA	durra
COLZA	a plant of the cabbage family	DURRA	a cereal grain
		EDEMA	excessive accumulation of serous fluid
COMA	condition of prolonged unconsciousness		
		ENEMA	a liquid injected into the rectum
COMMA	a fragment of a few words or feet in ancient prosody		
		ENTIA	existing or real things
CONGA	a Latin American dance	EPHA	ephah
COPRA	dried coconut meat	ERA	an epoch
COTTA	a short surplice	ERICA	shrub of the heath family
COXA	the hip or hip joint	ETA	a Greek letter
CULPA	negligence for which one is liable	ETNA	a container for heating liquids
CUPPA	a cup of tea	EXTRA	something additional

EYRA	a wild cat of tropical America	GUMMA	a soft tumor
FA	the fourth tone of the diatonic musical scale	GUTTA	a drop of liquid
		HA	a sound of surprise
FACIA	fascia	HALVA	halvah
FAENA	a series of passes made by a matador in a bullfight	HAMZA	an Arabic diacritical mark
		HENNA	to dye with a reddish coloring
FANGA	fanega – a dry measure	HERMA	a herm
FAUNA	the animal life of a particular region	HILA	of hilum
		HOLLA	to hallo
FELLA	a man or boy	HONDA	a part of a lariat
FERIA	a weekday of a church calendar on which no feast is celebrated	HOOKA	hookah
		HORA	an Israeli dance
		HULA	a Hawaiian dance
FETA	a Greek cheese	HUZZA	to cheer
FILA	threadlike structures	HYDRA	a freshwater polyp
FLEA	a parasitic insect	HYENA	a wolf like mammal
FLORA	the plant life of a particular region	HYLA	a tree frog
		HYPHA	a threadlike element of a fungus
FLOTA	a fleet of Spanish ships		
FOLIA	of folium	IDEA	a conception existing in the mind
FORA	of forum		
FOSSA	an anatomical depression	ILEA	of ileum
FOVEA	shallow anatomical depression	ILKA	each
		INFRA	below
FRENA	parts of a tongue	IOTA	a Greek letter
GAGA	crazy	ISBA	a Russian log hut
GALA	a celebration	IXIA	a flowering plant
GALEA	helmet shaped anatomical part	JAGRA	type of unrefined sugar
		JAVA	coffee
GAMBA	a bass viol	JNANA	knowledge acquired through meditation
GAMMA	Greek ornamental designs		
GANJA	cannabis used for smoking	JOTA	a Spanish dance
GEMMA	asexual reproductive structure	JUBA	a lively dance
		JUGA	yoke like structures
GENOA	a triangular sail	JUNTA	a governmental council
GIGA	a gigue	JURA	of jus
GLEBA	a spore-bearing mass of fungi	KA	spiritual self of a human being in Egyptian religion
GOA	an Asian gazelle	KAKA	a parrot
GONIA	point of lower jaw	KALPA	period of time in Hindu religion
GRAMA	a pasture grass		
GRANA	of granum	KANA	the Japanese syllabic script
GUAVA	a tropical shrub	KAPA	a coarse cloth

KAPPA	a Greek letter	LUNA	alchemical designation for silver
KARMA	force generated by a person's actions	LUTEA	pigment in fats and eggs
KASHA	a cooked cereal	LYCEA	of lyceum
KAVA	a tropical shrub	LYSSA	rabies
KEA	a parrot	LYTTA	fibrous band in the tongue of certain mammals
KHEDA	wild elephant enclosure		
KIBLA	kiblah	MA	mother
KIVA	underground ceremonial chamber	MAFIA	a secret organization in opposition to legal authority
KOA	a timber tree		
KOALA	an Australian mammal	MAGMA	the molten matter from which igneous rock is formed
KOLA	cola		
KAPPA	a Greek letter		
KRONA	a monetary unit of Iceland	MAMA	mother
KURTA	a shirt worn in India	MAMBA	a venomous snake
LA	sixth tone of the musical scale	MAMMA	mama or a milk secreting organ
LABIA	of labium	MANA	a supernatural force in certain Pacific island religions
LABRA	of labrum		
LAMA	a Buddhist monk		
LAMIA	a female demon	MANIA	an excessive interest
LARVA	immature form of various insects and animals	MANNA	divinely supplied food
		MANTA	a cotton fabric
LAURA	a type of monastery	MARIA	of mare
LAVA	molten rock from volcano	MASSA	master
LEA	a meadow	MATZA	matzo
LEHUA	a tropical tree	MAYA	the power to produce illusions in Hindu philosophy
LEMMA	a type of proposition in logic		
LIANA	a tropical vine	MBIRA	an African musical instrument
LIBRA	ancient Roman unit of weight		
		MECCA	a place visited by many people
LIMA	edible seed of a tropical plant	MEDIA	middle layer of a blood or lymph vessel
LIMBA	an African tree		
LINGA	lingam	MENSA	the grinding surface of a tooth
LIRA	a monetary unit of Italy		
LLAMA	a ruminant mammal	MENTA	of mentum
LOCA	of locus	MESA	a land formation having a flat top and steep sides
LOGIA	of logion		
LATA	telephone network	META	positions in a benzene ring separated by one carbon atom
LUFFA	type of sponge		

LATA

8

MICA	a mineral	OHIA	lehua - type of tree
MICRA	of micron	OKA	a Turkish unit of weight
MILIA	a gland secretion	OKRA	a tall annual herb
MILPA	field cleared from a jungle for farming purposes	OLEA	of oleum *OLEO*
		OLLA	a wide mouthed pot or jar
MINA	ancient unit of weight or value	OMEGA	a Greek letter
		OPERA	a form of musical drama
MIRZA	a Persian title of honor	ORA	of os
MOA	an extinct flightless bird	ORCA	orc
MOCHA	a choice pungent coffee	ORRA	occasional
MOIRA	fate or destiny in ancient Greek religion	OSSA	of os
		OSSIA	or else used as a musical direction
MOLA	a marine fish		
MOMMA	mother	OSTIA	of ostium
MOOLA	money	OVA	of ovum
MORA	unit of metric time in prosody	PA	a father
		PACA	a large rodent
MOXA	a Chinese plant	PACHA	pasha
MUDRA	a hand gesture in East Indian classical dancing	PAISA	a coin of Pakistan
		PALEA	a small bract
MULLA	mullah	PAMPA	a grassland of South America
MURA	a Japanese village		
MURRA	used to make fine vases and cups in ancient Rome	PANGA	a large knife
		PAPA	a father
MUSCA	any of a genus of flies	PARA	a monetary unit of Yugoslavia
MYNA	an Asian bird		
MYOMA	tumor composed of muscle tissue	PARKA	a hooded garment
		PASHA	a former Turkish high official
NA	not		
NANA	a grandmother	PASTA	a food made of dough
NEMA	a nematode	PEA	edible seed of an annual herb
NIPA	a palm tree		
NOMA	a severe inflammation of the mouth	PENNA	any of the feathers that determine a bird's shape
NONA	a virus disease	PHYLA	of phylon and phylum
NORIA	a type of waterwheel	PIA	a membrane of the brain
NOTA	of notum	PICA	a craving for unnatural food
NOVA	a type of star		
NUBIA	a woman's scarf	PIETA	representation of Virgin Mary mourning over body of Christ
NUCHA	the nape of the neck		
NYALA	an antelope		
OBIA	obeah	PIKA	a small mammal
OCA	a South American herb	PILEA	of pileum
OCREA	a sheathing plant part	PIMA	a strong high grade cotton

PINA	a pineapple	RIATA	a lasso
PINNA	feather wing or wing like part	ROTA	a roster
		RUGA	an anatomical folds or wrinkle
PINTA	a skin disease		
PITA	a strong fiber	RUMBA	a Cuban dance
PIZZA	an Italian open pie	RYA	Scandinavian hand woven rug
PLAYA	the bottom of a desert basin		
		SABRA	a native Israeli
PLAZA	a public square	SACRA	of sacrum
PLEA	an entreaty	SAGA	medieval Scandinavian narrative
PLENA	of plenum		
PLICA	a fold of skin	SAIGA	a small antelope
PODIA	of podium	SALPA	a free swimming tunicate
POLKA	a vivacious dance	SAMBA	to perform a Brazilian dance
POPPA	papa		
PRESA	a musical symbol	SANGA	fortifications
PRIMA	primo	SAUNA	a Finnish steam bath
PROA	prau	SCENA	an elaborate composition for a single voice
PRUTA	prutah		
PUCKA	pukka	SCHWA	a type of vowel sound
PUKKA	genuine	SCUBA	underwater breathing device
PUMA	a cougar		
PUNA	a cold arid plateau	SCUTA	of scutum
PUNKA	a ceiling fan used in India	SEA	the ocean
PUPA	stage of a metamorphic insect	SENNA	a medicinal plant
		SEPIA	a brown pigment
PURDA	purdah	SEPTA	of septum
PYA	a copper coin of Burma	SERA	of serum
QUA	in the capacity of	SETA	a coarse stiff hair
QUOTA	a proportional part or share	SHEA	an African tree
		SHIVA	a period of mourning
RAGA	a Hindu musical form	SIGMA	a Greek letter
RAIA	rayah	SILVA	sylva
RAJA	a ruler in India	SIMA	an igneous rock
RAYA	a person of authority	SIRRA	form of address
REATA	riata	SKUA	a predatory seabird
RECTA	a rectum	SODA	a type of chemical compound
REDIA	the larva of certain flatworms		
		SOFA	a long upholstered seat
REGMA	a type of fruit	SOFTA	a Muslim theological student
REGNA	of regnum		
RETIA	of rete	SOJA	the soybean
RHEA	a flightless bird	SOLA	of solum
RHYTA	ceremonial containers	SOMA	the body of an organism

SORA	a marsh bird	TESLA	a unit of magnetic induction
SOYA	soy		
SPA	a mineral spring	TESTA	hard outer coating of a seed
SPICA	an ear of grain		
SPUTA	of sputum	TETRA	a tropical fish
STELA	inscribed slab used as a monument	THECA	a poisonous alkaloid
		THETA	a Greek letter
STOA	ancient Greek covered walkway	THUJA	evergreen tree or shrub
		THUYA	thuja
STOMA	minute opening in the epidermis of a plant organ	TIARA	jeweled headpiece
		TIBIA	a bone of the leg
STRIA	a thin groove stripe or streak	TINEA	a fungous skin disease
		TOGA	outer garment worn in ancient Rome
STUPA	a Buddhist name		
SUBA	chief native officer in India	TOLA	a unit of weight used in India
SULFA	a bacteria inhibiting drug		
SUMMA	a comprehensive work	TONGA	a light cart used in India
SUPRA	above	TORA	torah
SURA	a chapter of the Koran	TRONA	a mineral
SURRA	a disease of domestic animals	TRYMA	a type of nut
		TSUBA	part of a Japanese word
SUTRA	a Hindu aphorism	TUBA	a brass wind instrument
SUTTA	sutra	TUFA	a porous limestone
SYLVA	the forest trees of an area	TUNA	a marine food fish
TA	an expression of gratitude	TWA	two
TABLA	a small drum	ULAMA	ulema
TAFIA	an inferior rum	ULEMA	a Muslim scholar
TAIGA	a subarctic evergreen forest	ULNA	a bone of the foreman
		ULTRA	an ultraist
TALA	a traditional rhythmic pattern of music in India	ULVA	an edible seaweed
		UMBRA	a dark area
TANKA	a Japanese verse form	UNCIA	a coin of ancient Rome
TAXA	of taxon	UREA	a chemical compound
TAZZA	an ornamental bowl	URSA	a female bear
TEA	a drink made by infusing dried leaves in hot water	USNEA	any of a genus of lichens
		UTA	any of a genus of large lizards
TECTA	dorsal parts of midbrain		
TEGUA	a type of moccasin	UVEA	a layer of the eye
TELA	an anatomical tissue	UVULA	pendent fleshy portion of the soft palate
TELIA	rust fungus		
TENIA	a tapeworm	VACUA	of vacuum
TEPA	a chemical compound	VANDA	a tropical orchid
TERGA	dorsal surface of insect	VARA	a Spanish unit of length
TERRA	earth land	VARIA	collection of literary works

VARNA	any of the four main Hindu social classes	ZOA	of zoon
VEENA	vina	ZOEA	a larval form of certain crustaceans
VELA	of velum		
VENA	a vein		
VERA	very		
VESTA	a short friction match		
VIA	by way of		
VILLA	an Roman agricultural estate		
VINA	a stringed instrument of India		
VINCA	a flowering plant		
VIOLA	a stringed instrument		
VIRGA	wisps of precipitation		
VISA	official endorsement on a passport		
VISTA	a distant view		
VITA	autobiographical sketch		
VITTA	a streak or band of color		
VIVA	a shout expressing approval		
VODKA	a liquor		
WALLA	wallah		
WEKA	a flightless bird		
WHA	who		
WHOA	command to stop an animal		
WIRRA	used to express sorrow		
WISHA	used to express surprise		
YA	you		
YEA	an affirmative vote		
YENTA	a gossipy woman		
YERBA	a South American beverage resembling tea		
YOGA	a Hindu philosophy involving physical discipline		
YUCCA	a tropical plant		
YUGA	an age of time in Hinduism		
ZAMIA	a tropical plant		
ZANZA	an African musical instrument		
ZEBRA	an African mammal		
ZETA	a Greek letter		

B

ACERB	sour	DARB	considered extraordinary
ALB	a long-sleeved-vestment	DAUB	to smear
AROEB	an Egyptian unit of capacity	DEB	a debutante
BARB	a sharp projection	DEMOB	discharge from military service
BIB	to tipple	DIB	fish by letting bob lightly on the water
BIBB	a mast support		
BLAB	to talk idly	DRAB	cheerless
BLEB	a blister	DRIB	to drip
BLOB	to splotch	DRUB	to beat severely
BLURB	a note on a book jacket	DUB	to confer knighthood on
BOB	to move up and down	DUMB	incapable of speech
BOMB	explosive projectiles	EBB	to recede
BOOB	a woman's breast	EXURB	a residential area beyond the suburbs of a city
BUB	young fellow		
BULB	an underground bud	FAB	
CAB	a taxicab	FIB	to tell a trivial lie
CABOB	kabob	FLAB	flabby body tissue
CAROB	an evergreen tree	FLUB	to bungle
CELEB	a celebrity; a famous person	FOB	to deceive
		FORB	an herb other than grass
CHIMB	the rim of a cask	FUB	to fob
CHUB	a fresh water fish	GAB	to chatter
CLIMB	to ascend	GAMB	a leg
CLOMB	a past tense of climb	GARB	to clothe
CLUB	an organized group	GIB	fasten with wedge of wood or metal
COB	a corncob		
COBB	a sea gull	GLIB	fluent
COMB	a toothed instrument	GLOB	a rounded mass
COOMB	combe – deep narrow valley	GOB	fill mine pit with waste materials
CRAB	to complain	GRAB	to grasp suddenly
CRIB	to confine closely	GRUB	to dig
CRUMB	small pieces	HERB	flowering plant with a non woody stem
CUB	the young of certain animals		
		HOB	to furnish with hobnails
CUBEB	a woody vine	HUB	the center of a wheel
CURB	to restrain	IAMB	a type of metrical foot
DAB	to touch lightly	JAB	to poke sharply

13

JAMB	to jam	SAB	to sob
JIB	to refuse to proceed further	SAHIB	master as a term of respect in colonial India
JIBB	shift fside to side while sailing	SCAB	crust that forms over a healing wound
JOB	to work by the piece	SCRUB	to rub hard in order to clean
KAB	Hebrew unit of measure	SHRUB	a low woody plant
KABAB	kabob	SIB	a sibling
KABOB	cubes of meat cooked on a skewer	SIBB	sib
KEBAB	kabob	SLAB	broad flat pieces of solid material
KEBOB	kabob	SLOB	a slovenly or boorish person
KERB	to provide with curbing	SLUB	to draw out and twist slightly
KNOB	a rounded protuberance	SLURB	poorly planned suburban area
LAB	a laboratory	
LAMB	a young sheep	SNIB	to latch
LIB	liberation	SNOB	one who tends to rebuff those regarded as inferior
LIMB	to cut off the arms or legs of	SNUB	treat with contempt or neglect
LOB	to throw or hit in a high arc	
MIB	a type of playing marble	SOB	to cry with a convulsive catching of the breath
MOB	to crowd about	SORB	take up and hold by absorption
NAB	to capture or arrest	
NABOB	one who is rich in India	SQUAB	a young pigeon
NAWAB	a nabob	SQUIB	to lampoon
NEB	the beak of a bird	STAB	pierce with a pointed weapon
NIB	to provide with a pen point	
NOB	a wealthy person	STOB	to stab
NUB	a protuberance or knob	STUB	to strike accidentally against a projecting object
NUMB	lacking sensation	
ORB	to form into a circle or sphere	SUB	to act as a substitute
		SWAB	clean with a large mop
PLEB	a commoner	SWOB	to swab
PLUMB	to determine depth of	TAB	to name or designate
PUB	a tavern	THROB	to pulsate
REB	a Confederate soldier	THUMB	the short thick digit of the human hand
RHOMB	a rhombus	
RHUMB	point on mariner's compass	TOMB	a burial vault or chamber
RIB	to poke fun at	TUB	a round open vessel
ROB	to take property from illegally	
RUB	move along the surface of a body with pressure	

KOB

VERB	a word used to express an act, or mode of being
WAB	a web
WEB	an interlaced fabric or structure
WOMB	the uterus

C

ADUNC	bent inward
ANTIC	to act in a clownish manner
ARC	to move in a curved course
ASDIC	sonar
ASPIC	the asp
ATTIC	a story or room directly below the roof of a house
AULIC	pertaining to a royal court
AURIC	pertaining to gold
AZOIC	geologic periods that precede the appearance of life
BARIC	pertaining to barium
BASIC	a fundamental
BLOC	a coalition
BORIC	pertaining to boron
BRONC	bronco
CERIC	containing cerium
CHIC	elegance
CIVIC	pertaining to a city
COLIC	acute abdominal pain
COMIC	a comedian
CONIC	a geometric curve
COSEC	cosecant
CUBIC	a mathematical equation or expression
CUSEC	unit of flow of liquids
CYNIC	a cynical person
DARIC	an ancient Persian coin
DISC	to disk
DOC	doctor
DOMIC	domical
DUC	a duke
DUROC	a large red hog
EPIC	a long narrative poem
ETHIC	a body of moral principles
EXEC	an executive officer
FISC	a state or royal treasury

FLIC	a Parisian policeman
FLOC	to aggregate into floccules
FRANC	a monetary unit of France
GAMIC	requiring fertilization
GENIC	pertaining to genes
HAVOC	to destroy
HEMIC	pertaining to blood
HIC	used to represent a hiccup
HUIC	used to encourage hunting hounds
HUMIC	derived from humus
ILEAC	pertaining to the ileum
ILIAC	pertaining to the ilium
IODIC	pertaining to iodine
IONIC	a style of type
LAC	substance secreted by insects
LAIC	a layman
LILAC	a flowering shrub
LINAC	device for imparting high velocities to charged particles
LOGIC	the science of reasoning
LOTIC	pertaining to moving water
LYRIC	a lyrical poem
LYTIC	pertaining to lysis
MAC	a raincoat
MAFIC	minerals rich in magnesium and iron
MAGIC	sorcery
MALIC	pertaining to apples
MANIC	one that is affected with mania
MARC	fruit residue after being pressed
MEDIC	one engaged in medical work:
MELIC	pertaining to song

16

MESIC	characterized by a medium supply of moisture	SUMAC	a flowering tree or shrub
MIMIC	to imitate closely	SYNC	to cause to operate in unison
MUSIC	sounds organized to produce a unified composition	TALC	soft mineral with soapy texture
NARC	an undercover drug agent	TAROC	a card game
ODIC	pertaining to an ode	TELIC	directed toward a goal
OLEIC	pertaining to oil	TIC	an involuntary muscular contraction
ONTIC	having a being or existence	TONIC	something that invigorates or refreshes
OPTIC	an eye		
ORC	a marine mammal	TOPIC	a subject of discourse
OTIC	pertaining to the ear	TORC	a metal collar or necklace
PAC	a shoe similar to a moccasin	TORIC	pertaining to a torus
		TOXIC	pertaining to a toxin
PANIC	to be overwhelmed by fear	TUNIC	a loose fitting garment
PIC	a photograph	TYPIC	typical
PUBIC	pertaining to the pubes or pubis	UMIAC	an Eskimo boat
		UREIC	pertaining to urea
PUDIC	pertaining to the pudendum	URIC	pertaining to urine
		VATIC	pertaining to a prophet
PYIC	pertaining to pus	VINIC	derived from wine
PYRIC	pertaining to burning	XEBEC	a Mediterranean sailing vessel
RABIC	pertaining to rabies		
REBEC	an ancient stringed instrument	XENIC	pertaining to a type of culture medium
REC	recreation	XERIC	requiring only a small amount of moisture
RELIC	a surviving memorial of something past		
		YOGIC	pertaining to yoga
ROC	a legendary bird of prey	ZEBEC	xebec
RUNIC	pertaining to a rune	ZINC	a metallic element
SAC	a pouch like structure in an animal or plant	ZOIC	pertaining to animals
SALIC	pertaining to a group of igneous rocks		
SEC	secant		
SERAC	a large mass of ice broken off of a glacier		
SIC	to urge to attack		
SONIC	pertaining to sound		
SPIC	a Spanish American person -an offensive term		
STOIC	indifferent to pleasure or pain		

17

D

ABED	in bed	BEND	to curve
ACID	type of chemical compound	BID	an offer of a price
		BIELD	to shelter
ACOLD	cold	BIFID	divided into two parts
ACRED	owning many acres	BIND	to tie or secure
ACRID	sharp and harsh smell	BIPED	a two-footed animal
AD	an advertisement	BIPOD	a two-legged support
ADD	to combine or join	BIRD	winged warm-blooded vertebrates
AHEAD	at to the front		
AHOLD	a hold or grasp of something	BLAND	soothing
		BLEED	lose blood
AID	to help	BLEND	mix smoothly and inseparably together
ALLOD	allodium		
ALMUD	Spanish unit of capacity	BLIND	sightless
ALOUD	audibly	BLOND	light colored
AMEND	to improve	BLOOD	fluid circulated by the heart
AMID	amide		
AND	added condition or stipulation	BOD	a body
		BOLD	daring
APHID	a small, soft-bodied insect	BOND	to join together
ARID	extremely dry	BOUND	to leap
AROID	a flowering plant	BOVID	a bovine
AUDAD	aoudad	BRAD	to fasten with thin nails
AULD	old	BRAID	to weave together
AVID	eager	BRAND	to mark with a hot iron
AVOID	to keep away from	BREAD	to cover with bread crumbs
AWARD	to grant as due or merited	BRED	past tense of bread
BAD	not good in any way	BREED	cause to give birth
BALD	lacking hair	BROAD	wide
BAND	to decorate with flexible strips of materials	BUD	undeveloped plant parts
		BUILD	to construct
BARD	to armor a horse	BUND	a political association
BAUD	unit of data transmission speed	BURD	a maiden
		CAD	an ungentlemanly man
BAWD	a madman	CAID	a Muslim leader
BEAD	round pieces of glass	CAIRD	a gypsy
BEARD	to oppose boldly	CARD	a stiff piece of paper
BED	to provide with a bed	CAULD	cold

CEBID	one of a family of monkeys	EMYD	a freshwater tortoise
CHAD	a scrap of paper	END	to terminate
CHARD	a variety of beet	EPHOD	an ancient Hebrew vestment
CHILD	a young person		
CHORD	a combination of three or more musical tones	FAD	a practice or interest that enjoys brief popularity
CLAD	coat one metal over another	FARAD	a unit of electrical capacitance
CLOD	a dolt	FARD	to apply cosmetics to
COD	a marine food fish	FAULD	a piece of armor below the breastplate
COED	a female student		
COLD	having little or no warmth	FED	a federal agent
CORD	a thin rope	FEED	to give food
COULD	past tense of can	FELID	a feline
CREED	a statement of belief	FEND	to ward off
CRIED	past tense of cry	FEOD	a fief
CROWD	to press into an insufficient space	FETID	having an offensive odor
		FEUD	a bitter, continuous hostility
CRUD	to curd		
CUD	food to be chewed again	FIO	a square bar used as a support for a topmast
CUPID	winged representative of the Roman god of love		
		FIELD	to play as a fielder
CURD	to curdle	FIEND	a demon
CYCAD	a tropical plant	FIND	to come upon after a search
DAD	father		
DEAD	deprived of life	FIORD	fjord
DEED	a legal document	FJELD	a high, barren plateau
DID	a past tense of do	FJORD	a narrow inlet of the sea between steep cliffs
DREAD	to fear greatly		
DRIED	past tense of dry	FLED	past tense of flee
DRUID	one of an ancient Celtic order of priests	FLIED	past tense of fly
		FLOOD	to inundate
DRYAD	a nymph of the woods	FLUID	a substance that tends to flow
DUAD	a pair		
DUD	a bomb that fails to explode	FOLD	to lay one part over another part of
DYAD	a pair of units	FOND	having affection for
EARED	having ears	FOOD	taken to maintain life
EGAD	used as a mild oath	FORD	to cross by wading
ELAND	a large antelope	FOUND	to establish
ELD	old age	FRAUD	trickery
EMBED	to fix firmly into a surrounding mass	FREED	past tense of free
		FREMD	strange
EMEND	to correct	FRIED	past tense of fry

19

FROND	a type of leaf	HERD	a group of animals
FUD	an old fashioned person	HEXAD	a group of six
FUND	to provide money for	HID	past tense of hide
GAD	to roam	HIND	a female red deer
GADID	gadoid	HOARD	to gather and store away
GAUD	a showy ornament	HOD	a portable trough
GED	a food fish	HODAD	a non-surfer
GELD	to castrate	HOLD	to maintain possession
GELID	icy	HOMED	past tense of home
GEOID	a hypothetical surface of	HOOD	a covering for the head
	the earth	HOUND	to pursue relentlessly
GID	a disease of sheep	HUMID	having much humidity
GILD	cover with a thin layer of	HYOID	a bone of the tongue
	gold	ICED	past tense of ice
GIRD	to surround	ID	part of the psyche
GLAD	feeling pleasure	ILIAD	a long poem
GLAND	a secreting organ	IMBED	to embed
GLEED	a glowing coal	IMID	imide
GOAD	drive animals with a	INNED	past tense of in
	pointed stick	IVIED	covered with ivy
GOD	a supernatural being	JEHAD	jihad
GOLD	a precious metallic element	JERID	Turkish equestrian sport
GONAD	a sex gland	JIHAD	a Muslim holy war
GOOD	having positive or desirable	KID	to tease
	qualities	KIND	having a gentle giving
GOURD	a hard shelled fruit		nature
GOWD	gold	KNEAD	to work into a uniform
GRAD	a graduate		mixture with the hands
GRAND	large and impressive	LAD	a boy or youth
GREED	excessive desire for wealth	LAID	past tense of lay
GRID	a grating	LAIRD	the owner of a landed
GRIND	to wear smooth, or		estate
	sharpen by friction	LAKED	process of releasing
GUARD	to protect		hemoglobin
GUID	good	LAND	solid ground
GUILD	association of people of	LARD	melted fat of hogs
	the same trade	LAUD	to praise
HAD	past tense of have	LEAD	to show the way to by
HALID	halide		going in advance
HAND	the end of the forearm	LED	past tense of lead
HARD	firm and unyielding	LEND	to give temporary use of
HEAD	to be chief of	LEUD	a feudal vassal
HEED	to pay attention to	LEWD	obscene
HELD	past tense of hold		

LIARD a former silver coin of France

LID a movable cover

LIPID any of a class of fatty substances

LIVID having the skin abnormally discolored

LOAD to place in or on

LORD a man of high rank

LOUD strongly audible

LUCID easily understood

LURID causing shock or horror

LYARD streaked with gray

MAD insane

MAID a maiden

MAUND an Asian unit of weight

MEAD an alcoholic beverage

MEED a deserved reward

MELD to blend

MENAD maenad

MEND to repair

MID the middle

MILD not harsh

MIND to heed

MOD one who wears bodily stylish clothes

MOLD to work into a particular shape

MONAD a single celled organism

MOOD a person's emotional state at a particular moment

MOPED a type of motorbike

MOULD to mold

MOUND to pile

MUCID musty

MUD soft wet earth

MURID a murine

MYOID resembling muscle

NAIAD a water nymph

NAKED being without clothing

NALED an insecticide

NARD a fragrant ointment

NEED to have an urgent or essential use for

NITID bright

NOD briefly lower the head forward

NOMAD a wanderer

OCTAD a group of eight

OD a hypothetical force of natural power

ODD one that is odd or unusual

OLD living or existing for a relatively long time

OOTID one of the four sections into which a mature ovum divide

OREAD a mountain nymph in Greek mythology

OUD a stringed instrument of northern Africa

OVOID an egg shaped body

OXID oxide

PAD to line or stuff with soft material

PAGOD pagoda

PAID past tense of pay

PARD a leopard

PAVID timid

PED a natural soil aggregate

PEND to remain undecided or unsettled

PIED past tense of pie

PILED past tense of pile

PLAID a woolen scarf of a checkered pattern

PLEAD to ask for earnestly

PLED past tense of plead

PLIED past tense of ply

PLOD to walk heavily

POD to produce seed vessels

POIND to seize and sell the property of to satisfy a debt

POND a body of water smaller than a lake

POOD a Russian unit of weight

21

POUND	to strike heavily and repeatedly	RYND	an iron support
PRIED	past tense of pry	SAD	unhappy
PROD	to jab with something pointed	SAID	past tense of say
PROUD	having or displaying pride	SALAD	a dish of green raw vegetables
PUD	pudding	SAND	a loose granular rock material
PYOID	puslike	SAPID	pleasant to the taste
QAID	caid – a Muslim leader	SARD	a variety of quartz
QUAD	space out by means of quadrats	SAROD	a lute of northern India
QUID	a portion of something to be chewed	SAYID	sayyid – title of respect
QUOD	a prison	SCAD	a marine fish
RABID	effected with rabies	SCALD	to burn with hot liquid or steam
RAD	to fear	SCEND	to rise upward as on a wave
RAID	to make a sudden assault on	SCOLD	to rebuke harshly
RAND	a strip of leather at the heel of a shoe	SCROD	a young cod
		SCUD	to run or move swiftly
RANID	any of a large family of frogs	SEED	propagative plant structure
		SEND	a silk fabric
RAPID	moving or acting with great speed	SHAD	a food fish
		SHARD	a fragment of broken pottery
READ	to look at so as to take in the meaning	SHED	a small low structure
RED	color of blood	SHEND	to disgrace
REDO	to put in order	SHERD	shard
REED	the stalks of tall grass	SHIED	past tense of shy
REND	to tear apart forcibly	SHOD	past tense of shoe
RESID	a type of fuel oil	SHRED	to tear into small strips
RID	to tree from something objectionable	SIDED	past tense of side
		SILD	a young herring
RIGID	not flexible	SKALD	an ancient Scandinavian poet
RIND	a thick and firm outer covering	SKID	to slide sideways as a result of a loss of traction
ROAD	an open way for public passage	SKIED	past tense of ski and sky
		SLED	a vehicle for carrying loads over snow or ice
ROD	a straight slender piece of wood or other material	SLOID	sloyd
		SLOJD	sloyd
ROOD	a large crucifix	SLOYD	a Swedish system of manual training
ROSED	past tense of rose	
ROUND	shaped like a sphere	
RUDD	a freshwater fish	SNED	to prune

22

SNOOD	a net or fabric cap for the hair	TIMID	lacking courage or self confidence
SOD	turf	TOAD	a tailless jumping amphibian
SOLD	past tense of sell		
SOLID	having definite shape and volume	TOO	a British unit of weight
		TOLD	past tense of tell
SORD	a flight of mallards	TRAD	traditional
SOUND	being in good health or condition	TREAD	to walk on over or along
		TREND	to take a particular course
SPED	past tense of speed	TRIAD	a group of three
SPEED	to move swiftly	TRIED	past tense of try
SPEND	to payout	TROD	past tense of tread
SPIED	past tense of spy	TUMID	swollen
SPUD	remove with a spade like tool	TURD	a piece of dung
		TWEED	a coarse woolen fabric
SQUAD	small organized groups	UNBID	unbidden
SQUID	ten armed marine mollusks	UNDID	past tense of undo
STAID	sober and sedate	UPEND	to set or stand on end
STAND	to assume or maintain an upright position	UPPED	past tense of up
		URD	an annual bean grown in India
STEAD	to be of advantage to		
STEED	a horse	VALID	evidence that can be supported
STIED	past tense of sty		
STOOD	past tense of stand	VAPID	insipid
STUD	to set thickly with small projections	VELD	veldt
		VEND	to sell
SUDD	a floating mass of vegetation	VIAND	an article of food
		VIRID	verdant
SURD	a voiceless speech sound	VIVID	strikingly bright or intense
SWARD	to cover with turf	VOID	of no legal force or effect
SWORD	a weapon having a long blade for cutting or thrusting	WAND	a slender rod
		WARD	to turn aside
		WEALD	a woodland
SYNOD	a church council	WED	to marry
TABID	progressive bodily wasting	WEED	undesirable plants
TAD	a small boy	WEIRD	mysteriously strange
TED	to spread for drying	WELD	to join by applying heat
TEIID	a tropical American lizard	WEND	to proceed along
TEIND	a tithe	WHID	to move rapidly and quietly
TEND	to be disposed or inclined	WIELD	to handle or use effectively
TEPID	moderately warm	WILD	living in a natural state uncultivated area
THIRD	one of three equal parts		
THUD	to make a dull heavy sound	WIND	to pass around an object or fixed center

VID

WOAD	a blue dye
WOALD	a yellow pigment
WOLD	an elevated tract of open land
WOOD	the hard, fibrous substance beneath the bark of a tree
WORD	speech sounds that communicate meaning
WORLD	the earth and all its inhabitants
WOULD	past tense of will
WOUND	to inflict an injury
WRIED	past tense of wry
WUD	insane
WYND	a narrow street
YAIRD	a garden
YALD	yauld
YARD	land adjacent to a building
YAUD	an old mare
YAULD	vigorous
YELD	not giving milk
YID	a Jew - an offensive term
YIELD	to give up
YIRD	earth
YOD	a Hebrew letter
YOND	yonder
ZED	the letter Z
ZOOID	an organic cell or body capable of independent movement

ABASE	to lower in rank, prestige, or esteem
ABATE	to reduce in degree or intensity
ABBE	an abbot
ABELE	Eurasian Tree
ABIDE	to accept without objection
ABLE	having sufficient power, skill, or resources
ABODE	a dwelling place
ABOVE	something that is in a higher place
ABUSE	to use wrongly or improperly
ABYE	to make amends
ACE	score a point in a single stroke
ACHE	suffer a dull, continuous pain
ACME	the highest point
ACNE	a skin disease
ACRE	unit of area
ACUTE	marked by sharpness or severity
ADAGE	traditional saying expressing a common
ADDLE	confuse
ADOBE	an un-burnt, sun-dried brick
ADORE	to love deeply
ADOZE	dozing
ADZE	adz
AE	one
AERIE	a bird's nest built high on a mountain or cliff
AFIRE	being on fire
AFORE	before

AGAPE	the love of God for mankind
AGATE	variety of quartz
AGAVE	a tropical plant
AGAZE	gazing
AGE	to grow old
AGEE	to one side
AGENE	chemical compound used in bleaching flour
AGGIE	a type of playing marble
AGILE	able to move quickly and easily
AGLEE	agley
AGONE	ago
AGREE	to have the same opinion
AGUE	a malarial fever
AIDE	an assistant
AINE	brilliant, happiness
AINEE	aine
AISLE	a passageway between sections of seats
AJEE	awry
AKEE	a tropical tree
AKENE	achene
ALAE	a wing
ALANE	alone
ALATE	having wings
ALME	almah
ALOE	an African plant
ALONE	apart from others
AMAZE	to overwhelm with surprise or wonder
AMBLE	to saunter
AMICE	a vestment won about the neck and shoulders
AMIDE	a type of chemical compound
AMIE	a female friend

AMINE	a type of chemical compound	AWARE	having perception or knowledge
AMOLE	a plant root used as a substitute for soap	AWE	reverential fear
		AWEE	awhile
AMPLE	abundant	AWOKE	a past tense of awake
AMUSE	to occupy pleasingly	AXE	to ax
ANE	one	AXILE	axial
ANELE	to anoint	AXITE	a fiber of an axon
ANGLE	to fish with a hook and line	AXLE	a shaft upon which a wheel revolves
ANILE	resembling an old woman		
ANIME	a resin obtained from a tropical fish	AXONE	axon
		AYE	an affirmative vote
ANISE	North African plant	AZIDE	a type of chemical compound
ANKLE	the joint connecting the foot and leg		
		AZOLE	a type of chemical compound
ANODE	a positively charged electrode		
		AZOTE	nitrogen
ANOLE	a tropical lizard	AZURE	a blue color
ANTE	to put a fixed into the pot before the cards are dealt	BABE	a baby
		BADE	past tense of bid
ANTRE	a cave	BADGE	to supply with a insignia
APACE	swiftly	BAIZE	a green, woolen fabric
APE	to mimic	BAKE	to prepare food in an oven
APPLE	an edible fruit	BALE	to form into tightly compressed bundles
APSE	a domed, semicircular projection of a building		
		BANE	to kill with poison
ARE	unit of surface measure	BARBE	a medieval cloth headdress
ARETE	a flowering plant	BARDE	to bard
ARGLE	to argue	BARE	naked
ARGUE	to present reason for or against	BARGE	a long, large boat
		BARRE	to playa type of guitar chord
ARISE	to get up		
AROSE	past tense of arise	BARYE	a unit of pressure
ARSE	the buttocks-usually considered vulgar	BASE	morally low
		BASTE	to sew loosely together
ASIDE	a comment intended to be heard only by the audience	BATE	to reduce the force of
		BATHE	to wash
ATE	blind impulse or ambition that drives one to ruin	BE	to exist
		BEE	a winged insect
ATONE	to make amends or reparation	BEIGE	a tan color
		BELIE	misrepresent
AVE	expression of greeting or farewell	BELLE	an attractive woman
		BENE	benne
AWAKE	to wake up	BENNE	the sesame plant

BERME	berm	BOULE	a pear shaped gem
BIBLE	an authoritative publication	BOUSE	to haul by means of a tackle
BICE	a blue or green pigment	BOWSE	bouse – a stock exchange
BIDE	to wait	BRACE	to support
BIKE	to bicycle	BRAE	a hillside
BILE	a fluid secreted by the liver	BRAKE	to slow down or stop
BILGE	to spring a leak	BRAVE	showing courage
BINE	a twining plant stern	BRAZE	to solder together
BINGE	a drunken carousal	BREDE	a braid
BIOME	an ecological community	BREE	broth
BIRLE	to' carouse	BREVE	a symbol used to indicate a short vowel
BIRSE	a bristle		
BISE	a cold wind	BRIBE	to practice bribery
BITE	to seize with the teeth	BRIDE	a woman just married or about to be married
BITTE	please		
BIZE	bise	BRIE	a mold ripened cheese
BLADE	a cutting edge	BRINE	salted water
BLAE	bluish-black	BROKE	past tense of break
BLAME	to find fault with	BROME	a tall grass
BLARE	to sound loudly	BROSE	a porridge
BLASE	indifferent	BRUME	fog
BLATE	timid	BRUTE	shape a diamond by rubbing it with another diamond
BLAZE	to burn brightly		
BLITE	an annual herb		
BLOKE	a fellow	BUDGE	to move slightly
BLUE	having the color of the clear sky	BUGLE	a brass wind instrument
		BUGLE	to swell out
BLUME	to blossom	BURKE	to murder by suffocation
BLYPE	a shred	BURSE	a small bag or pouch
BOCCE	boccie	BUTTE	an isolated hill
BOCHE	a German a derogatory term	BYE	a side issue
		BYRE	a cowshed
BODE	to be an omen	BYTE	group of adjacent binary digits
BOGIE	bogy		
BOGLE	a bogy	CABLE	heavy rope
BOITE	a nightclub	CACHE	to store in a hiding place
BOLE	a fine clay	CADE	a European shrub
BOMBE	a frozen dessert	CADGE	to get by begging
BONE	to debone	CADRE	a nucleus of trained personnel
BONNE	a housemaid		
BONZE	a Buddhist monk	CAFE	a restaurant
BOOZE	to drink liquor excessively	CAGE	to confine
BORE	to pierce with a rotary tool		

CAKE	to form into a hardened mass	CHYME	semi-digested food
CALVE	to give birth to calf	CINE	a motion picture
CAME	a leaden window rod	CITE	to quote as an example
CANE	to beat with a rod	CIVIE	civvy
CANOE	a light, slender boat	CLAVE	a past tense of cleave
CAPE	a sleeveless garment	CLEPE	to call by name
CARE	to be concerned or interested	CLIME	climate
CARLE	a peasant or farmer	CLINE	a series of changes within a species
CARSE	low, fertile land along a river	CLONE	reproduce by asexual means
CARTE	a menu	CLOZE	pertaining to a type of reading comprehension test
CARVE	to form by cutting		
CASE	a container or receptacle	CLUE	to give guiding information
CASTE	system of distinct social classes	COBLE	a small fishing boat
		CODE	to convert into symbols
CATE	a choice food	COKE	to change into a carbon fuel
CAUSE	to bring about		
CAVE	to hollow out	COLE	a plant of the cabbage family
CAVIE	a hencoop		
CEASE	cacique	COMBE	a narrow valley
CEDE	to yield	COME	to move toward something or someone
CEE	the letter C		
CENSE	to perfume with incense	COMTE	a French nobleman
CERE	to wrap in a waxy cloth	CONE	a geometric shape
CETE	a group of badgers	CONGE	permission to depart
CHAFE	to warm by rubbing	CONTE	a short story
CHAPE	a part of scabbard	COOEE	to cry out shrilly
CHARE	to do small jobs	COPE	to contend or strive
CHASE	to pursue	COPSE	a coppice
CHIDE	to scold	CORE	the central part
CHILE	chili	CORSE	a corpse
CHIME	ring harmoniously	COSIE	a cozy
CHINE	to cut through the backbone	COUDE	pertaining to a type of telescope
CHIVE	an herb used as a seasoning	COUPE	an automobile with two doors
CHOKE	to impede the breathing of	COVE	to curve over or inward
CHORE	to do small jobs	COZIE	cozy
CHOSE	an item of personal property	CRAKE	a small harsh-voiced bird
		CRANE	to stretch out one's neck
CHUTE	a vertical passage	CRAPE	to crepe
CHYLE	a digestive fluid	CRATE	to put in a packing box

CRAVE	to desire greatly	DENSE	compact
CRAZE	to make insane	DERE	dire
CREME	cream	DEUCE	to bring a tennis score to a tie
CREPE	fabric with crinkled surface		
CRIME	a violation of the law	DHOLE	a wild dog of India
CRONE	a withered old woman	DICE	to cut into small cubes
CRORE	a monetary unit of India	DIE	to cease living
CROZE	a toot used in barrel-making	DIENE	a chemical compound
		DIKE	to furnish with an embankment
CRUDE	unrefined		
CRUSE	a small bottle	DIME	a coin of the United States
CUBE	a regular solid	DINE	to eat dinner
CUE	to give a signal to an actor	DIODE	a type of electron tube
CUKE	a cucumber	DIRE	disastrous
CURE	to restore to health	DIRGE	a funeral song
CURIE	a unit of radioactivity	DISME	a former coin of the United States
CURSE	to wish evil upon		
CURVE	to deviate from straightness	DITE	a small amount
		DIVE	to plunge headfirst into water
CUTE	pleasingly attractive		
CUTIE	a cute person	DOBIE	abode
CYCLE	to ride a bicycle	DODGE	to evade
CYME	a flower cluster	DOE	a female deer
DACE	a freshwater fish	DOGE	the chief magistrate in former republic of Venice
DALE	a valley		
DAME	a matron	DOGIE	a stray calf
DANCE	to move rhythmically to music	DOLCE	a soft toned organ stop
		DOLE	distribute in small portions
DARE	to have the necessary courage	DOME	a rounded roof
		DONE	past participle of do
DATE	statement of calendar time	DONEE	a recipient of a gift
DAUBE	a braised meat stew	DOPE	to give a narcotic to
DAZE	to stun	DOSE	specified quantity of medicine
DE	used in names and phrases		
DEAVE	to deafen	DOTE	to show excessive affection
DEBYE	a unit of measure for electric dipole moments	DOUCE	sedate
		DOUSE	to plunge into water
DEE	the letter D	DOVE	a bird of the pigeon family
DEICE	to free from ice	DOWIE	dreary
DEKE	to feint in hockey	DOWSE	to search for underground water with a divining rod
DELE	to delete		
DELVE	to search in depth	DOXIE	doxy
DEME	a Greek district	DOZE	to sleep lightly
DENE	a valley	DRAKE	a male duck

DRAPE	to arrange in graceful folds	ELITE	a socially superior group
DRAVE	past tense of drive	ELOPE	to run of secretly to be married
DREE	to suffer		
DRIVE	to urge or propel forward	ELSE	in a different place time or way
DRONE	to make a continuous low sound		
		ELUDE	to evade
DROVE	to drive cattle or sheep	ELUTE	remove by means of a solvent
DRUPE	a fleshy fruit		
DRUSE	a crust of small crystals lining a rock cavity	EMCEE	serve as master of ceremonies
DUCE	a leader	EME	an uncle
DUDE	a dandy	EMOTE	to express emotion in an exaggerated manner
DUE	something that is owed		
DUKE	a high-ranking nobleman	EMYDE	emyd - tortoise
DULSE	an edible seaweed	ENATE	a relative on the mother's side
DUNCE	a stupid person		
DUNE	a hill of sand	ENDUE	to provide with some quality or grit
DUPE	to deceive		
DUPLE	having two parts or elements	ENSUE	to occur afterward or as a result
DURE	to endure	ENURE	to inure
DWINE	to pine or waste away	EPEE	a type of sword
DYE	a coloring material or matter	EPODE	a type of poem
		ERASE	to rub or scrape out
DYKE	to dike	ERE	previous to before
DYNE	a unit of force	ERNE	a sea eagle
EAGLE	a large bird of prey	ERODE	wear away by constant friction
EAGRE	a tidal flood		
EASE	to give rest of relief to	EROSE	uneven
EAVE	lower projecting edge of a roof	ETAPE	a warehouse
		ETUDE	a piece of music
ECHE	to increase	ETWEE	etui
ECOLE	a French school	EVADE	escape or avoid by cleverness or deceit
EDGE	a bounding or dividing line		
EDILE	aedile –a Roman magistrate	EVE	evening
		EVITE	to avoid
EDUCE	to draw forth or bring out	EVOKE	to call forth
EERIE	weird	EWE	a female sheep
EIDE	of eidos – formal content of a culture	EXILE	to banish from one's own country
		EXINE	the outer layer of certain spores
EKE	to supplement with great effort		
		EYE	to watch closely
ELATE	to raise the spirits of	EYNE	of eye
ELIDE	to omit		

EYRE	a journey	FIQUE	a tropical plant
EYRIE	aerte	FIRE	project by discharging a gun
FABLE	to compose or tell fictitious tales	FIVE	a number
FACE	to oppose or meet defiantly	FLAKE	flat, thin pieces
FADE	to lose color or brightness	FLARE	to bum with a bright, wavering light
FADGE	to succeed	FLEE	to run away
FAKE	to contrive and present as genuine	FLITE	to quarrel
FALSE	contrary to the truth or fact	FLOE	a large mass of floating ice
FAME	to make famous	FLUE	an enclosed passageway for directing a current
FANE	a temple	FLUKE	to obtain by chance
FARCE	to fill out with witty material	FLUME	to convey by means of an artificial water channel
FARE	to get along	FLUTE	a woodwind instrument
FARLE	farl – thin circular cake	FLYTE	flite – a dispute or scolding
FATE	to destine	FOE	an enemy
FAUVE	a fauvist	FOGLE	fogy
FAZE	to disturb the composure of	FORCE	to overcome resistance by the exertion of strength
FEASE	to faze	FORE	the front part of something
FEAZE	to faze	FORGE	to fashion or reproduce for fraudulent purposes
FEE	a fixed charge	FORGE	to refrain from
FEEZE	to faze	FORME	an assemblage of printing type secured in a metal frame
ˮFEME	a wife		
FEMME	a woman		
FENCE	to practice the art of fencing	FORTE	a strong point
FERE	a companion	FOSSE	a ditch
FESSE	a horizontal band across the middle of a shield	FRAE	from
		FRAME	to construct by putting together the various parts
FETE	to honor with a celebration	FREE	not subject to restriction
FIBRE	fiber	FRERE	brother
FICE	a feist – a small dog	FRISE	frieze
FICHE	a sheet of microfilm	FROE	a cleaving tool
FIDGE	to fidget	FRORE	frozen
FIE	used to express disapproval	FROZE	past tense of freeze
		FUDGE	to falsify
FIFE	a high-pitched flute	FUGLE	to lead
FILE	an abrading tool	FUGUE	a type of musical composition
FILLE	a girl		
FINE	of excellent quality	FUME	gaseous exhalations

ʼɛʃ

FURZE	a spiny shrub	GLAZE	to fit windows with glass panes
FUSE	a detonating device		
FUSEE	a large headed friction match	GLEBE	the soil or earth
		GLEDE	a bird of prey
FUZE	fuse	GLEE	an unaccompanied song
FUZEE	fusee	GLIDE	to move effortlessly
FYCE	feist – a small dog	GLIME	to glance slyly
FYKE	a bag shaped fishnet	GLOBE	to form into a perfectly round body
FYTTE	a division of a poem or song		
		GLOVE	hand coverings
GABLE	a triangular section of a wall	GLOZE	to explain away
		GLUE	an adhesive substance
GAE	to go	GLUME	a bract on grassy plants
GAFFE	a social blunder	GNOME	a dwarf
GAGE	to pledge as security	GONE	departed
GALE	a strong wind	GOOSE	a swimming bird
GAMBE	gamb	GORE	to pierce with a horn or tusk
GAME	to gamble		
GANE	past participle of gae	GORGE	to stuff with food
GAPE	to stare with open mouth	GORSE	furze
GATE	a movable barrier	GOUGE	to cut or scoop out
GAUGE	to measure precisely	GRACE	to give beauty to
GAUZE	a transparent fabric	GRADE	to arrange in steps or degrees
GAVE	past tense of give		
GAZE	to look intently	GRAPE	an edible berry
GEE	to turn to the right	GRATE	to reduce to shreds by rubbing
GEESE	of goose		
GELEE	a cosmetic gel	GRAVE	extremely serious
GENE	a hereditary unit	GRAZE	to feed on growing grass
GENIE	jinni	GREBE	a diving bird
GENRE	a type or kind	GREE	to agree
GEODE	a type of rock	GRIDE	to scrape harshly
GESTE	gest	GRIME	to make dirty
GHEE	a liquid butter made in India	GRIPE	to grasp
		GROPE	to feel about with the hands
GIBE	to jeer		
GIE	to give	GROVE	a small forested area
GIGUE	a lively dance	GRUME	a thick viscid substance
GIVE	to transfer freely to another	GUDE	good
		GUIDE	to show the way to
GLACE	to cover with icing	GUILE	to beguile
GLADE	an open space in a forest	GUISE	to disguise
GLARE	shine with a harsh brilliant light	GURGE	to swirl

GYBE	to shift from side to side while sailing	HOPE	to have desire or expectation
GYRE	to move in a circle or spiral	HORDE	to gather in a large group
GYVE	to shackle	HORSE	a large hoofed mammal
HADE	to incline	HOSE	to spray with water
HAE	to have	HOUSE	a building in which people live
HAKE	a marine fish		
HALE	healthy or compel to go	HOVE	past tense of heave
HALVE	to divide into two equal parts	HOWE	a valley
		HOYLE	a rule book
HAME	a part of a horse collar	HUE	color
HANCE	side of an arch	HUGE	very large
HANSE	a guild of merchants	HYPE	a deception
HAOLE	one who is not a native Hawaiian	HYTE	insane
		ICE	frozen water
HARE	to run	IDLE	inactive or to pass time idly
HASTE	to hasten	IMAGE	a reproduction of someone
HATE	to despise	IMBUE	to make thoroughly wet
HAVE	to be in possession of	IMIDE	a chemical compound
HAWSE	a part of a ship's bow	IMINE	a chemical compound
HAZE	to subject to a humiliating initiation	INANE	nonsensical or empty space
		INBYE	within
HE	a male person	INDUE	to endue
HEAVE	to lift forcefully	INGLE	a fire
HEDGE	to surround with a hedge	INKLE	a tape used for trimming
HEEZE	to hoist	INURE	to accustom to accept something undesirable
HELVE	to provide with a handle		
HEME	a component of hemoglobin	IRADE	a decree of a Muslim ruler
		IRATE	angry
HENCE	consequently	IRE	to anger
HERE	this place	IRONE	an aromatic oil
HIDE	concealed; obscure	ISLE	a small island
HIE	to hurry	ISSUE	to come forth
HIKE	to walk a long distance	ISTLE	a strong fiber
HINGE	to attach a jointed device	IXTLE	istle
HIRE	to engage the services of for payment	JADE	to weary
		JAKE	all right; fine
HIVE	a bee's nest	JAMBE	a jambeau
HOE	a gardening tool	JANE	a girl or woman
HOISE	to hoist	JAPE	to mock
HOKE	to give false value to	JEE	to gee
HOLE	a cavity in a solid	JEFE	a chief
HOME	place of residence	JESSE	to jess
HONE	to sharpen	JETE	a ballet leap

H EBE

33

JIBE	to gibe	LADE	to load with a cargo
JIVE	to play jazz or swing music	LADLE	a type of spoon
JOE	a fellow	LAKE	a sizable inland body of water
JOKE	to say something amusing		
JOLE	jowl	LAME	physically disabled
JOULE	a unit of energy	LANCE	a spear like weapon
JUBE	a platform in a church	LANE	a narrow passageway
JUDGE	to decide on critically	LAPSE	to fall from a previous standard
JUICE	liquid of a fruit or vegetable		
		LARGE	considerable size or quantity
JUKE	to fake out of position		
JUPE	a woman's jacket	LASE	to function as a laser
JUTE	a strong coarse fiber	LATE	coming or occurring after the expected time
KAE	a bird resembling a craw		
KALE	a variety of cabbage	LATHE	to cut or shape on a type of machine
KAME	a mound of detrital material		
		LAVE	to wash
KANE	kain	LAZE	to pass time lazily
KEDGE	to move a vessel with the use of an anchor	LEASE	to grant temporary use of in exchange for rent
KEEVE	a tub or vat	LEAVE	to go away from
KERNE	a medieval foot soldier	LEDGE	a narrow shelf like projection
KIBE	a sore caused by exposure to cold		
		LEE	a shelter from the wind
KIKE	a Jew – offensive term	LENSE	lens
KINE	a type of television tube	LEONE	a monetary unit of Sierra Leone
KITE	to obtain money or credit fraudulently		
		LETHE	forgetfulness
KITHE	to make known	LEVEE	an embankment
KNAVE	a dishonest person	LIANE	liana
KNEE	a joint of the leg	LICE	of louse
KNIFE	a sharp-edged instrument used for cutting	LIE	to speak falsely
		LIEGE	a feudal lord
KOINE	a type of dialect	LIEVE	gladly
KOPJE	a small hill	LIFE	the quality that distinguishes animals and plants from inanimate matter
KRONE	a monetary unit of Denmark		
KUE	the letter Q		
KYRIE	a religious petition for mercy	LIKE	to find pleasant
		LIME	a calcium compound
KYTE	the stomach	LINE	slender continuous marks
KYTHE	to make visible	LISLE	a fine tightly twisted cotton thread
LACE	a cord for drawing together two edges		
		LITHE	bending easily

LITRE	liter	LYRE	an ancient harp like instrument
LIVE	function as an animal or plant	LYSE	to cause to undergo lysis
LIVRE	former monetary unit of France	MACE	a club like weapon
		MACLE	a spot or discoloration in a mineral
LOBE	a rounded projecting anatomical part	MADE	past tense of make
LODE	a deposit of ore	MADRE	mother
LODGE	to furnish with temporary quarters	MAE	more
		MAGE	a magician
LOGE	a small compartment	MAHOE	a tropical tree
LONE	having no companions	MAILE	a Pacific island vine
LONGE	to guide a horse by means of a long rope	MAIZE	an American cereal grass
		MAKE	to cause to exist
LOOIE	lieutenant of the armed forces	MALE	individual that begets young by fertilizing the female
LOOSE	not firm taut or rigid		
LOPE	to run with a steady easy gate	MAMMY	a black nursemaid
		MANE	long hair growing about the neck of some animals
LORE	traditional knowledge or belief	MANGE	a skin disease of domestic animals
LOSE	to come to be without and be unable to find		
		MANSE	a clergyman's house
LOUIE	looie	MAPLE	a hardwood tree
LOUPE	a small magnifying glass	MARE	a mature female horse
LOUSE	a parasitic insect	MARGE	a margin
LOVE	to feel great affection for	MARSE	master
LOWE	to blaze	MASSE	a type of shot in billiards
LOWSE	loose	MATE	partners in a union
LUBE	a lubricant	MATTE	to produce a dull finish on
LUCE	a freshwater fish	MAUVE	a purple color
LUCRE	monetary gain	MAVIE	a song thrush
LUNE	a crescent shaped figure	MAYBE	possibly
LUNGE	to make a forceful forward movement	MAZE	to bewilder
		ME	I
LURE	to attract with something desirable	MELEE	a confused struggle
		MENSE	to do honor to
LUTE	a stringed musical instrument	MERE	a pond or lake
		MERGE	to combine
LUXE	luxury	MERLE	a blackbird
LYASE	an enzyme	MESNE	being between two extremes
LYCEE	a French secondary school		
LYE	a solution used in making soap	METE	to distribute by measure
		METRE	to meter

MICE	of mouse	MUTE	characterized by an absence of speech
MIDGE	a small winged insect		
MIKE	a microphone	MYOPE	one who is affected with myopia
MILE	a unit of distance		
MILLE	a thousand	NACRE	the pearly internal layer of certain shells
MIME	to mimic		
MINCE	to cut into very small pieces	NAE	not
		NAIVE	lacking sophistication
MINE	to dig into for valuable materials	NAME	to give a title
		NANCE	an effeminate male
MIRE	to cause to stick in swampy ground	NAPE	the back of the neck
		NAPPE	a type of rock formation
MISE	an agreement or settlement	NAVE	the main part of a church
		NEE	born with the name of
MITE	a small arachnid	NENE	a Hawaiian goose
MITRE	to miter	NERVE	to give courage to
MODE	a method of doing or acting	NEUME	a sign used in musical notation
MOIRE	a fabric having a wavy pattern	NEVE	a granular snow
		NGWEE	a Zambian unit of currency
MOKE	a donkey	NICE	pleasing to the senses
MOLE	a small burrowing animal	NICHE	a receding space or hollow
MOME	a fool	NIDE	to nest
MONDE	the world	NIECE	a daughter of one's brother or sister
MONIE	many		
MONTE	a card game	NIEVE	the fist of a hand
MOOSE	a ruminant mammal	NINE	a number
MOPE	to act in a dejected or gloomy manner	NITRE	niter
		NIXIE	a female water sprite
MORE	a greater amount	NOBLE	possessing qualities of excellence
MOSTE	past tense of mote		
MOTE	a small particle	NODE	a swollen enlargement
MOTTE	a small growth of trees on a prairie	NOISE	to spread as a rumor or report
MOUE	a pouting grimace	NOME	a province of modem Greece
MOUSE	a small rodent		
MOVE	to change from one position to another	NONCE	the present occasion
		NONE	one of seven canonical daily periods for prayer
MOVIE	a motion picture		
MOXIE	spirit of courage	NOOSE	to secure with a type of loop
MULE	a sterile hybrid		
MURE	to immure	NOPE	no
MURRE	a diving bird	NOSE	the organ of smell
MUSE	to ponder	NOTE	to write down

NUDE	being without clothing or covering	OUTRE	deviating from what is usual or proper
NUDGE	to push gently	OVATE	egg shaped
NUDIE	a movie featuring nude performers	OVINE	a sheep or a closely related animal
NUKE	a nuclear weapon	OVULE	a rudimentary seed
NURSE	to care for the sick or infirm	OWE	to be under obligation to pay
OBE	obeah	OWSE	ox
OBESE	very fat	OXEYE	a flowering plant
OBOE	a woodwind instrument	OXIDE	a binary compound of oxygen with another element
OBOLE	a coin of medieval France		
OCHRE	to ocher		
ODE	a lyric poem	OXIME	a chemical compound
ODYLE	a hypothetical force	OZONE	a form of oxygen
DE	a whirlwind off the Faeroe Islands	PACE	to walk with a regular step
		PADLE	a hoe
OGEE	shaped molding	PAGE	to summon by calling out the name of
OGIVE	a pointed arch		
OGLE	to stare at	PAISE	of paisa
OGRE	a monster	PALE	lacking intensity of color
OKE	oka	PANE	a sheet of glass for a window
OLDIE	popular song of an earlier day		
		PANNE	a lustrous velvet
OLE	a shout of approval	PARGE	to parget
OLIVE	the small oval fruit of a Mediterranean tree	PARLE	to parley
		PARSE	to describe and analyze grammatically
OMBRE	a card game		
ONCE	one single time	PARTE	to cut off the outer covering of
ONE	a number		
OORIE	ourie	PARVE	made without milk or meat
OOZE	to flow or leak out slowly	PASE	a movement of a matador's cape
OPE	to open		
OPINE	to hold or state as an opinion	PASSE	outmoded
		PASTE	to fasten with a sticky mixture
ORATE	to speak formally		
ORE	a mineral or rock containing a valuable metal	PATE	the top of the head
		PAUSE	to stop temporarily
ORLE	a heraldic border	PAVE	to cover with material that forms a firm level surface
OSE	an esker		
OUNCE	a unit of weight	PAYEE	one to whom money is paid
OUPHE	an elf		
OURIE	shivering with cold	PE	a Hebrew letter
		PEACE	to be or become silent

37

PEAGE	peag	POLE	long thin piece of wood or metal
PEASE	a pea		
PEE	to urinate sometimes considered vulgar	POME	a fleshy fruit with a core
		PONE	a com bread
PEEVE	to annoy	POPE	the head of the Roman Catholic Church
PEISE	to weigh		
PEKE	a small long haired dog	PORE	to gaze intently
PEKOE	a black tea	POSE	to assume a fixed position
PELE	a medieval fortified tower	POSSE	a body of men summoned to aid a peace officer
PENCE	of penny		
PERE	a father	PRASE	a mineral
PERSE	a blue color	PRATE	to chatter
PEWEE	a small bird	PREE	to test by tasting
PHAGE	an organism that destroys bacteria	PRESE	of presa
		PRICE	to set a value on
PHASE	distinct stages of development	PRIDE	a feeling of self esteem
		PRIME	to make ready
PHONE	to telephone	PRISE	to raise or force with a lever
PHYLE	a political subdivision in ancient Greece		
		PRIZE	to value highly
PICE	a former coin of India and Pakistan	PROBE	to investigate or examine thoroughly
PIE	to pi	PROLE	a member of the working class
PIECE	to join into a whole		
PIKE	a long spear	PRONE	lying with the front or face downward
PILE	to lay one upon the other		
PINE	to yean intensely	PROSE	writing without metrical structure
PIPE	a hollow cylinder		
PIQUE	to arouse anger or resentment	PROVE	to establish the truth
		PRUDE	a prudish person
PIXIE	pixy	PRUNE	to cut off branches
PLACE	to set in a particular position	PUCE	a dark red color
		PUKE	to vomit
PLAGE	a bright region on the sun	PULE	to whine
PLANE	to make smooth or even	PULSE	to pulsate
PLATE	coat with a thin layer of metal	PURE	free from anything different inferior or contaminating
PLEBE	a freshman at a military or naval academy		
		PUREE	to reduce to a thick pulp by cooking and sieving
PLIE	a movement in ballet		
PLUME	to cover with feathers	PURGE	to purify
POISE	to hold in a state of equilibrium	PURSE	to pucker
		PYE	a book of ecclesiastical rules in the English church
POKE	to push or prod		

PYRE	a pile of combustible material	REE	the female Eurasian sandpiper
PYXIE	an evergreen shrub	REEVE	to fasten by passing through or around something
QUAKE	to shake or vibrate		
QUALE	a property considered apart from things having the property	REIVE	to plunder
		RENTE	annual income under French law
QUARE	queer		
QUATE	quiet	RETE	an anatomical mesh
QUEUE	to line up	REVUE	a type of musical show
QUITE	to the fullest extent	RHYME	verse with corresponding terminal sounds
QUOTE	to repeat the words of		
RACE	a contest of speed	RICE	to press through a ricer
RAGE	to act or speak with violent anger	RIDE	to be conveyed by an animal or machine
RAISE	to move to a higher position	RIDGE	long narrow elevations
		RIFE	abundant
RAKE	to gather with a toothed implement	RIFLE	to search through and rob
		RILE	to anger
RAKEE	Turkish brandy	RILLE	a valley on the moon's surface
RALE	an abnormal respiratory sound		
		RIME	to rhyme
RAMEE	ramie	RINSE	to cleanse with clear water
RAMIE	an Asian shrub	RIPE	fully developed
RANCE	a variety of marble	RISE	to move upward
RANGE	to place in a particular order	RITE	a ceremonial act or procedure
RAPE	to force to submit to sexual intercourse	RIVE	to tear apart
		ROBE	a long loose outer garment
RAPHE	a seam like ridge between two halves of an organ	ROBLE	an oak tree
		RODE	past tense of ride
RARE	occurring infrequently	ROE	the mass of fish eggs
RASE	to raze	ROGUE	to defraud
RATE	to estimate the value of	ROLE	a part played by an actor
RATHE	appearing or ripening early	ROOSE	to praise
RAVE	to speak irrationally	ROPE	a thick line of twisted fibers
RAZE	to tear down or demolish	ROSE	a reddish flower
RAZEE	to make lower by removing the upper deck as a ship	ROTE	mechanical routine
		ROUE	a lecherous man
RE	the second tone of the diatonic musical scale	ROUGE	to color with a red cosmetic
		ROUSE	bring out a state of sleep
REAVE	to plunder	ROUTE	to send on a particular course
REBBE	a rabbi		
REDE	to advise		

ROVE	to roam	SCREE	a mass of rocks at the foot of a slope
RUBLE	a monetary unit of Russia		
RUCHE	a pleated strip of fine fabric	SCUTE	a horny plate or scale
RUDE	discourteous or impolite	SEDGE	a marsh plant
RUE	feel sorrow or remorse for	SEE	to perceive
RUFFE	a freshwater fish	SEGUE	to proceed without pause from one theme to another
RULE	to exercise control over		
RUNE	a letter of an ancient alphabet	SEINE	to catch fish with a large vertically hanging net
RUPEE	a monetary unit of India		
RUSE	a deception	SEISE	to seize
RYE	a cereal grass	SEIZE	to take hold of suddenly and forcibly
RYKE	to reach		
SABE	to savvy	SELLE	a saddle
SABLE	a carnivorous mammal	SEME	a type of ornamental
SABRE	to saber	SENSE	to perceive by the senses
SADE	a Hebrew letter	SERE	withered dry
SADHE	sade	SERGE	a twilled fabric
SAE	so	SERVE	to work for
SAFE	free from danger	SHADE	to screen from light or heat
SAGE	wise	SHAKE	to move to and fro with short rapid movements
SAICE	syce – a stableman		
SAKE	benefit interest or advantage	SHALE	a fissile rock
		SHAME	a painful sense of guilt of degradation
SALE	the act or an instance of selling		
		SHAPE	outward form
SALVE	to soothe	SHARE	use in common with another or others
SAME	resembling in every relevant respect		
		SHAVE	to sever the hair close to the roots
SANE	mentally sound		
SAREE	sari	SHE	a female person
SARGE	sergeant	SHINE	to emit light
SATE	to satiate	SHIRE	a territorial division of Great Britain
SAUCE	a flavorful liquid dressing		
SAUTE	fry in a small amount of fat	SHIVE	a thin fragment
SAVE	to rescue from danger	SHOE	a covering for the foot
SCALE	to climb up or over	SHONE	past tense of shine
SCAPE	to escape	SHORE	to prop with a supporting timber
SCARE	to frighten		
SCENE	the place where some action or event occurs	SHOTE	shoat
		SHOVE	to push roughly
		SHUTE	to chute
SCONE	a flat round cake	SICE	syce
SCOPE	extent	SIDE	to agree with or support
SCORE	to make a point in a game	SIDLE	to move sideways

SIEGE	to attempt to capture or gain	SOUSE	to immerse
SIEVE	to pass through a sieve	SPACE	to set some distance apart
SIKE	syke – kidding, joking	SPADE	a digging implement
SINCE	from then until now	SPAE	to foretell
SINE	a trigonometric function	SPAKE	past tense of speak
SINGE	to bum slightly	SPALE	a splinter or chip
SIPE	to seep	SPARE	to refrain from punishing harming or destroying
SLUE	to cause to move sideways	SPATE	a freshet
SLYPE	a narrow passage in an English cathedral	SPICE	an aromatic vegetable substance
SMAZE	an atmospheric mixture of smoke and haze	SPIKE	a long thick nail
SMILE	to upturn the comers of the mouth in pleasure	SPILE	to stop up with a wooden plug
SMITE	to strike heavily	SPINE	the vertebral column
SMOKE	the gaseous product of burning materials	SPIRE	to rise in a tapering manner
SMOTE	past tense of smile	SPITE	to treat with malice
SNAKE	a limbless reptile	SPODE	a fine china
SNARE	to trap	SPOKE	rods that support the rim of a wheel
SNIDE	maliciously derogatory	SPORE	asexual usually single celled reproductive bodies
SNIPE	to shoot at individuals from a concealed place	SPREE	an unrestrained indulgence in an activity
SNORE	breathe loudly while sleeping	SPRUE	a tropical disease
SNYE	side channel in a river or creek	SPUE	to spew
SOAVE	an Italian wine	SPUME	to foam
SOCLE	a block used as a base for a column or pedestal	STADE	an ancient Greek unit of length
SOKE	a feudal right to administer justice	STAGE	to produce for public view
SOLE	the bottom surface of a shoe	STAKE	a pointed piece of wood or metal
SOLVE	to find the answer or explanation	STALE	not fresh
		STANE	to stone
SOME	being an unspecified number	STARE	to gaze fixedly
		STATE	to set forth in words
SONDE	a device for observing atmospheric phenomena	STAVE	to drive or thrust away
		STELE	central portion of vascular tissue in a plant stem
SONE	a unit of loudness	STERE	a unit of volume
SORE	painfully sensitive to the touch	STILE	a series of steps for passing over a fence or wall
		STIME	a glimpse

STIPE	slender supporting part of a plant	SYNE	since
STOKE	to supply a furnace with fuel	TABLE	a piece of furniture having a flat upper surface
STOLE	a long wide scarf	TACE	tasse
STONE	pieces of concreted earthy or mineral matter	TACHE	a clasp or buckle
		TAE	prep to
STOPE	to excavate in layers as ore	TAKE	to get possession of
STORE	to put away for future use	TALE	a story
STOVE	a heating apparatus	TAME	gentle or docile
STUPE	a medicated cloth to be applied to a wound	TAPE	a long narrow strip or band
		TARE	to determine the weight of a container holding goods
STYE	an inflamed swelling of the eyelid	TARGE	a small round shield
STYLE	to name	TARRE	to urge to action
SUAVE	smoothly affable and polite	TASSE	tasset
SUCRE	a monetary unit of Ecuador	TASTE	to perceive the flavor of by taking into the mouth
SUE	to institute legal proceedings	TATE	a tuft of hair
		TAUPE	a dark gray color
SUEDE	to finish leather with a soft napped surface	TAWIE	docile
		TAWSE	to flog
SUITE	a series of things forming a unit	TEASE	to make fun of
		TEE	place a golf ball on a small peg
SUPE	actor without a speaking part	TELE	a television set
SURE	free from doubt	TENSE	taut
SURGE	to move in a swelling manner	TEPEE	a conical tent of some North American Indians
SWAGE	to shape with a hammering tool	TERCE	tierce
		TERNE	an alloy of lead and tin
SWALE	a tract of low marshy ground	TERSE	succinct
		THAE	these, those
SWARE	past tense of swear	THANE	a man holding land by military service in old England
SWEDE	a rutabaga		
SWINE	a domestic pig		
SWIPE	to strike with a sweeping blow	THE	used to specify or make particular
SWIVE	to copulate with	THEE	the objective case of the pronoun thou
SWORE	past tense of swear		
SYCE	a male servant in India	THEME	a subject discussed in speech or writing
SYCEE	fine in-coined silver formerly used in China as money		
		THERE	at or in that place
		THESE	of this
SYKE	a small stream		

THINE	a possessive form of the pronoun thou	TOWIE	a form of contract bridge for three players
THOLE	to endure	TRACE	to follow the course of
THOSE	of that	TRADE	to give in exchange for another commodity
THREE	a number		
THROE	a violent spasm of pain	TRAVE	a frame for confining a horse
THYME	an aromatic herb		
TIDE	the rise and fall of the ocean's waters	TREE	a tall woody plant
		TRIBE	a group of people with common ancestry or culture
TIE	to fasten with a cord or rope		
TIKE	tyke	TRICE	to haul up with a rope
TILDE	a mark placed over a letter to indicate its sounds	TRINE	to place in a particular astrological position
TILE	thin slabs of baked clay	TRIPE	a part of the stomach
TIME	to determine the speed or duration of	TRITE	used so often as to be made commonplace
TINE	to lose	TRODE	past tense of tread
TINGE	a trace of color to	TROKE	to exchange
TIRE	to grow tired	TRONE	a weighing device
TITHE	a small tax	TROPE	the figurative use of a word
TITLE	a distinctive appellation	TROVE	a valuable discovery
TITRE	titer	TRUCE	to suspend hostilities by mutual agreement
TOE	one of the terminal members of the foot		
		TRUE	consistent with fact or reality
TOGUE	a freshwater fish		
TOILE	a sheer linen fabric	TSADE	sade
TOKE	a puff on a marijuana cigarette	TUBE	a long hollow cylinder
		TULE	a tall marsh plant
TOLE	to allure	TULLE	a silk material
TOME	a large book	TUNE	to put into the proper pitch
TONE	a sound of definite pitch & vibration	TUQUE	a knitted wool cap
		TUTEE	one who is being tutored
TONNE	a unit of weight	TWAE	two
TOPE	to drink liquor to excess	TWICE	two times
TOPEE	a pith helmet	TWINE	to twist together
TOPHE	tufa	TYE	a chain on a ship
TOQUE	a close fitting woman's hat	TYEE	a food fish
TORE	a torus	TYKE	a small child
TORSE	a wreath of twisted silks	TYNE	to tine
TORTE	a rich cake	TYPE	to write with a typewriter
TOTE	to carry by hand	TYRE	a covering for a wheel
TOUSE	to tousle	TYTHE	to tithe
		UKASE	an edict

UKE	ukulele	VIDE	used to direct a reader to another item
UNBE	to cease to have being	VIE	to strive for superiority
UNCLE	the brother of one's father or mother	VILE	physically
UNDE	wavy	VINE	a climbing plant
UNDEE	unde	VISE	a clamping device
UNDUE	exceeding what is appropriate or normal	VIVE	an exclamation of approval
UNITE	to bring together to form a whole	VOE	a small bay, creek or inlet
		VOGIE	vain
UNTIE	free from something that tie	VOGUE	the current trend or style
		VOICE	to express or utter
UPBYE	a little farther on	VOILE	a sheer fabric
URARE	curare	WACKE	a type of basaltic rock
URASE	urease	WADE	to walk through water
URATE	a chemical salt	WAE	woe
URGE	to force forward	WAGE	to engage in or carry on
URINE	liquid containing body waste	WAIVE	to give up intentionally
		WAKE	to rouse from sleep
USAGE	a firmly established and generally accepted practice	WALE	to mark with welts
		WAME	the belly
USE	to put into service	WANE	to decrease in size or extent
USQUE	type of whiskey		
UTILE	useful	WARE	to beware of
VAGUE	not clearly expressed	WASTE	to use thoughtlessly
VALE	a valley	WAVE	to move freely back and forth or up and down
VALSE	a concert waltz		
VALUE	the quality that renders a thing useful or desirable	WE	term referring to speaker and others
VALVE	a device for controlling the flow of a liquid or gas	WEAVE	to form by interfacing threads
		WEDGE	tapering piece of wood or metal
VANE	a device for showing the direction of the wind		
		WEE	a short time
VARVE	a deposit of sedimentary material	WERE	2nd person past tense on be
		WHALE	large marine mammals
VASE	a rounded decorative container	WHEE	used to express delight
		WHERE	the place at or in which something is located or occurs
VEE	the letter V		
VENGE	to avenge		
VENUE	the locale of an event	WHILE	to cause to pass pleasantly
VERGE	to come near	WHINE	a plaintive, high pitched sound
VERSE	to versify		
VERVE	vivacity	WHITE	of the color of pure snow
VICE	to vise		

WHOLE	all the parts making up a thing	YOWE	a ewe
		YOWIE	a small ewe
WHORE	to consort with prostitutes	YULE	a Christmas tree
WHOSE	the possessive case of who	ZAIRE	a monetary unit of Zaire
WIDE	having great extent from side to side	ZEE	the letter Z
		ZONE	areas distinguished from other adjacent areas
WIFE	a woman married to a man		
WILE	to entice	ZOWIE	expression of surprise or pleasure
WINCE	to flinch		
WINE	fermented juice of the grape	ZYME	an enzyme
WINZE	a steeply inclined mine shaft		
WIPE	to rub lightly in order to clean		
WIRE	a slender rod, strand, or thread of ductile		
WISE	to become aware or informed		
WITE	to blame		
WITHE	to bind with flexible twigs		
WIVE	to marry a woman		
WOE	tremendous grief		
WOKE	paste tense of wake		
WORE	past tense of wear		
WORSE	bad in a greater degree		
WOVE	past tense of weave		
WRITE	to form characters on a surface with an instrument		
WROTE	past tense of write		
WYE	the letter Y		
WYLE	to beguile		
WYTE	blame, fault		
YARE	nimble		
YE	you		
YINCE	once		
YIPE	used to express fear or surprise		
YODLE	to yodel		
YOGEE	yogi		
YOKE	wooden frame for joining together draft animals		
YORE	past		
YOUSE	you		

F

AFF	off	DUFF	a thick pudding
ALOOF	distant in interest or feeling	DWARF	extremely small
		EF	the letter F
ARF	used to express the bark of a dog	EFF	el
		ELF	a small often mischievous fairy
BAFF	to strike under a golf ball	FEOFF	to grant a fief to
BARF	to vomit	FIEF	a feudal estate
BEEF	a steer or cow fattened for food	FLUFF	to make fluffy
BIFF	to hit	GAFF	to catch a fish with a sharp hook
BLUFF	to mislead	GANEF	a thief
BOFF	a hearty laugh	GANOF	ganef – a scoundrel
BRIEF	short	GLIFF	a type of aircraft
BUFF	to polish	GOLF	a type of ball game
BUMF	paperwork	GONIF	ganef
CALF	a young cow or bull	GONOF	ganef
CALIF	caliph	GOOF	to blunder
CHAFF	to poke fun at	GRIEF	intense mental distress
CHEF	a chief cook	GRIFF	vein of gold ore
CHIEF	highest in authority	GRUFF	low and harsh in speech
CHUFF	gruff	GUFF	foolish talk
CLEF	a musical symbol	GULF	to swallow up
CLIFF	a high, steep face of rock	HAAF	a deep sea fishing ground
COFF	to buy	HALF	one of two equal parts
COIF	to style the hair	HOOF	the hard covering on the feet of certain animals
COOF	a dolt		
CORF	a wagon used in a mine	HOWF	a place frequently visited
CUFF	a part of a sleeve	HOWFF	howl
CUIF	cool	HUFF	to breathe heavily
CURF	incision made by a cutting tool	IF	a possibility
		JIFF	jiffy
DAFF	to thrust aside	KAIF	kef
DEAF	lacking the sense of hearing	KALIF	caliph
		KEEF	kef
DELF	delft	KEF	hemp smoked to produce euphoria
DOFF	to take off		
DRAFF	the damp remains of malt after brewing	KENAF	an East Indian plant

KAF (handwritten, next to JIFF/KAIF)

DEF (handwritten, left margin)
DIF (handwritten, left margin next to DELF/DOFF)

KERF	to make an incision with a cutting tool	SCURF	scaly or shredded dry skin
KIEF	kef	SELF	the total essential or particular being of one person
KIF	kef		
KLOOF	a ravine	SERF	a feudal slave
LEAF	a usually green flattened organ of vascular plants	SERIF	fine line used to finish off the main stroke of a letter
LIEF	willing	SHEAF	to sheave
LOAF	a shaped mass of bread	SHELF	a flat rigid structure used to support articles
LOOF	the palm of the hand		
LUFF	to steer a sailing vessel nearer into the water	SKIFF	a small open boat
		SLUFF	to discard a card or cards
MIFF	to annoy	SNIFF	to inhale audibly through the nose
MOTIF	a recurring thematic element in an artistic work		
		SNUFF	powdered tobacco
MUFF	to bungle	SPOOF	to hoax
NAIF	a naive person	STAFF	a body of assistants
NEIF	naive	STIFF	difficult to bend or stretch
OAF	a clumsy stupid person	STUFF	to fill or pack tightly
OF	coming from	SURF	to ride breaking waves on a long narrow board
OFF	to go away		
PELF	money or wealth	SWARF	material removed by a cutting tool
PILAF	dish made of seasoned rice		
POUF	a loose roll of hair	TEFF	a cereal grass
POUFF	pouf	THIEF	one that steals
PROF	a professor	TIFF	to have a petty quarrel
PROOF	to examine for errors	TOFF	a dandy
PUFF	to blow in short gusts	TREF	unfit for use according to Jewish law
QUAFF	to drink deeply		
QUIFF	a forelock	TUFF	a volcanic rock
RAFF	riffraff	TURF	layer of dense growth of grass and its roots
REEF	to reduce the area of a sail		
REF	to referee		
REIF	robbery	WAFF	to wave
RIFF	to riffle	WAIF	to throw away
ROOF	the external upper covering of a building	WHARF	a landing place for vessels
		WHIFF	to blow or convey with slight gusts of air
RUFF	to trump		
SCARF	a piece of cloth worn for warmth or protection	WOLF	a carnivorous mammal
		WOOF	to utter a gruff barking sound
SCOFF	to express rude doubt or derision		
		YAFF	to bark
SCUFF	walk without lifting the feet	ZARF	metal coffee cup holder

R I F

47

G

ACING	small saclike division of a gland	COHOG	a quahog
AGOG	in a state of eager curiosity	COLOG	the logarithm of the reciprocal of a number
ALANG	along	CRAG	a rough rock
ALMUG	a precious wood mentioned in the bible	CUING	a present participle of cue
ALONG	onward	DAG	a hanging end or shred
AMONG	in the midst of	DANG	to damn
AWING	a present participle of awe	DEBUG	to remove insects from
BAG	a flexible container	DEFOG	to remove from fog
BANG	to hit sharply	DIG	to turn over or remove earth
BEFOG	to envelop on fog	DING	to ring
BEG	to plead	DOG	a domesticated mammal
BEING	something that exists	DOING	an action
BERG	an iceberg	DONG	a deep sound of a large bell
BEWIG	to adorn with a wig	DRAG	to pull along the ground
BHANG	the hemp plant	DREG	the sediment of liquors
BIG	considerable size	DRUG	a medicinal substance
BOG	to impede	DUG	the udder of a female mammal
BONG	to make a deep, ringing sound	DUNG	to fertilize with manure
BOURG	a medieval town	DYING	a passing out of existence
BRAG	first-rate	EGG	to incite or urge
BRIG	a two-masted ship	ENG	a phonetic symbol
BRING	to take with oneself to a place	ERG	a unit of work or energy
BUG	to annoy	EYING	a present participle of eye
BUNG	to plug with a cork or stopper	FAG	to make weary by hard work
BURG	a city or town	FANG	a long pointed tooth
CHANG	a cattie	FIG	to adorn
CHUG	to move with a dull sound	FLAG	a piece of cloth used as a symbol
CLAG	to clog	FLING	to throw with force
CLANG	to ring loudly	FLOG	to beat with a whip or rod
CLING	to adhere closely	FLONG	a sheet of a type of paper
CLOG	to block up or obstruct	FLUNG	past tense of fling
CLUNG	past tense of Cling	FOG	condensed water vapor near the earth's surface
COG	to cheat at dice		

48

FRAG	injure with a type of grenade
FRIG	copulate - considered vulgar
FROG	web-footed, tailless amphibians
FRUG	a type of vigorous dance
FUG	to make stuffy and odorous
GAG	to pledge as security
GANG	a group
GIG	fish with a prolonged spear
GLEG	alert
GLOGG	an alcoholic beverage
GOING	an advance toward an objective
GONG	a disk-shaped percussion instrument
GRIG	a lively person
GROG	a mixture of liquor and water
HAG	to hack
HANG	to attach from above only
HOG	to take more than one's share
HOGG	a young sheep
HONG	a Chinese factory
HUG	to clasp tightly in the arms
HUNG	past tense of hang
HYING	present participle of hie
ICING	a sweet topping for cakes
INCOG	a disguised person
IRING	present participle of ire
JAG	to cut unevenly
JAGG	to jag
JIG	to bob
JUG	container with a narrow mouth and a handle
KEG	a small barrel
KIANG	a wild ass
KING	a male monarch
KLONG	a canal
LAG	to stay or fall behind
LANG	long

LEG	appendages that serve as a means of support
LIANG	a Chinese unit of weight
LING	a health plant
LOG	to cut down trees for timber
LONG	extending for a considerable distance
LUG	to carry or pull with effort
LUNG	a respiratory organ
MAG	a magazine
MIG	a type of playing marble
MIGG	mig
MOG	to move away
MUG	to assault with intent to rob
MUGG	to make funny faces
NAG	to find fault incessantly
NOG	a strong ale
NOGG	nog
OPING	present participle of ope
ORANG	a large ape
PANG	cause to have spasms of pain
PEAG	wampum
PEG	a wooden pin
PIG	cloven hoofed mammals
PING	a brief high pitched sound
PIROG	a large Russian pastry
PLUG	material used to fill a hole
PRANG	to cause to crash
PRIG	to steal
PROG	prowl for food or plunder
PRONG	pierce with a pointed projection
PUG	to fill in with clay or mortar
PUNG	a box shaped sleigh
QUAG	a quagmire
RAG	to scold
RANG	past tense of ring
RENIG	to renege
RIG	to put in proper condition
RING	a circular band
RUG	to tear roughly

49

RUING	present participle of rue	STUNG	past tense of sting
RUNG	a step of a ladder	SUING	present participle of sue
SAG	sink downward from weight	SWAG	stolen property
		SWANG	past tense of swing
SANG	past tense of sing	SWIG	to drink deeply or rapidly
SCAG	heroin	SWING	to move freely back and forth
SCRAG	to wring the neck of		
SHAG	to make shaggy	SWUNG	past tense of swing
SHOG	to move along	TAG	an identifying marker
SHRUG	to raise and contract the shoulders	TANG	provide with a pungent flavor
SING	to utter with musical inflections of the voice	TEG	a yearling sheep
		THING	an inanimate object
SKAG	heroin	THONG	strip of leather used for binding
SKEG	timber connecting the keel and stem post of a ship		
		THUG	a brutal ruffian or assassin
SLAG	fused residue of smelted ore	TING	to emit a high pitched metallic sound
SLANG	harsh or coarse language	TOG	to clothe
SLING	throw with a sudden motion	TONG	a type of grasping device
		TRIG	neat
SLOG	to plod	TUG	to pull with force
SLUG	to strike heavily	TUNG	a Chinese tree
SLUNG	past tense of sling	TWANG	a sharp vibrating sound
SMUG	highly self-satisfied	TWIG	to observe
SNAG	a jagged protuberance	TYING	present participle of tie
SNUG	warmly comfortable	UNPEG	to remove the pegs from
SONG	a musical composition written or adapted for singing	UNRIG	to divest of rigging
		VANG	a rope on a ship
		VEG	a vegetable
SPANG	directly	WAG	to move briskly up and down or to and fro
SPRAG	a device to prevent a vehicle from rolling backward		
		WHANG	to beat with a whip
SPRIG	to fasten with small thin nails	WIG	an artificial covering of hair for the head
		WING	organs of flight
SPRUG	a sparrow	WRANG	a wrong
SQUEG	oscillate in an irregular manner	WRING	to twist so as to compress
		WRONG	not according to what is right, proper, or correct
STAG	attend a function without a female companion		
		WRUNG	past tense of wring
STAIG	a colt	YANG	the masculine active principle in Chinese cosmology
STANG	to sting		
STING	to prick painfully		

YEGG	a burglar
ZAG	to turn sharply
ZIG	to turn sharply
ZING	to move with a high-pitched humming sound

H

AAH	to exclaim in amazement, joy, or surprise
ABASH	to make embarrassed
AH	used to express delight, relief, or contempt
AIRTH	a direction
AITCH	the letter H
ALMAH	Egyptian girl who sings and dances professionally
ALMEH	almah
AMAH	an Oriental nurse
ANKH	Egyptian symbol of enduring life
APISH	slavishly or foolishly imitative
ARCH	a curved structure spanning an opening
ASH	the residue of a substance that has been burned
AWASH	covered with water
AYAH	a native maid or nurse in India
AZOTH	mercury
BACH	to live as a bachelor
BAH	an exclamation of disgust
BAITH	both
BASH	to smash
BATCH	to bring together
BATH	a washing
BEACH	to drive ashore
BEECH	a type of tree
BELCH	to expel gas through the mouth
BENCH	to take a player out of game
BERTH	to provide with a mooring
BETH	a Hebrew letter
BIMAH	bema

BIRCH	to whip
BIRTH	to originate
BITCH	to complain
BLAH	nonsense
BOOTH	a small enclosure
BOSH	nonsense
BOTCH	to bungle
BOTH	being the two
BOUGH	a tree branch
BRACH	a hound bitch
BRASH	rash hasty
BROTH	a thin clear soup
BRUGH	a borough
BRUSH	to touch lightly
BUNCH	to group together
BURGH	a Scottish borough
BUSH	shrubs
BUTCH	a lesbian with mannish traits
CAPH	kaph
CASH	ready money
CATCH	to capture after pursuit
CHETH	heth
CINCH	to girth
CLACH	clachan – a small village
CLASH	to conflict or disagree
COACH	to tutor or train
CONCH	a marine mollusk
COACH	a sinuous dance
COSH	to bludgeon
COUCH	to put into words
COUGH	expel air from the lungs noisily
COUTH	sophisticated
CRASH	to collide noisily
CRUSH	press or squeeze out of shape

CRWTH	an ancient stringed musical instrument	FLUSH	ruddy
		FOH	faugh
CUISH	cuisse	FORTH	onward in time or place
CULCH	an oyster bed	FRESH	new
CURCH	a kerchief	FRITH	firth
CUTCH	catechu	FROSH	a freshman
DAH	a dash in Morse code	FROTH	to foam
DASH	to strike violently	GALAH	a cockatoo
DEASH	to remove ash from	GARTH	a yard or garden
DEATH	the end of life	GASH	to make a long deep cut in
DEPTH	deepness	GERAH	a Hebrew unit of weight
DISH	a concave vessel	GIRSH	qirsh – a monetary unit
DITCH	long narrow excavation	GIRTH	to encircle
DOETH	3rd person singular of do	GLYPH	an ornamental groove
DOTH	a present 3rd person of do	GNASH	to grind the teeth together
DOUGH	a flour mixture	GOSH	exclamation of surprise
DUNCH	a push	GRAPH	to represent using a diagram
DUTCH	each person paying for himself	GRITH	sanctuary for a limited period of time
EACH	being one of two or more distinct individuals	GULCH	a deep narrow ravine
EARTH	soil	GUSH	to flow forth forcefully
EATH	easy	HAH	ha
EDH	an old English letter	HARSH	severe
EH	used to express doubt	HASH	to mince
EPHAH	a Hebrew unit of dry measure	HATCH	bring forth young from an egg
EPOCH	a particular period of time	HATH	present 3d person sing of have
ETCH	to engrave with acid		
ETH	edh	HAUGH	a low-lying meadow
FAITH	to believe or trust	HEATH	an evergreen shrub
FASH	to annoy	HEIGH	used to attract attention
FAUGH	used to express disgust	HETH	a Hebrew letter
FETCH	to go after and bring back	HEUCH	heugh – shaft in coal mine
FIFTH	one of five equal parts	HIGH	reaching far upward
FILCH	to steal	HITCH	to fasten with a knot or hook
FILTH	foul or dirty matter		
FINCH	a small bird	HOOCH	cheap whiskey
FIRTH	an inlet of the sea	HORAH	hora
FISH	cold-blooded aquatic vertebrates	HOTCH	to wiggle
		HUH	used to express surprise
FITCH	a polecat	HUMPH	to utter a grunt
FLASH	a sudden burst of light	HUNCH	to arch forward
FLESH	soft body tissue	HUSH	to quiet

HUTCH	to store away	MACH	ratio of the speed of a body to the speed of sound
ICH	a disease of certain fishes		
INCH	to move very slowly	MARCH	to walk in a formal military manner
ITCH	tingling skin sensation		
JOSH	to tease	MARSH	a tract of low wet land
KAPH	a Hebrew letter	MASH	to reduce to a pulpy mass
KENCH	a bin for salting fish	MATCH	to set in competition
KETCH	a sailing vessel	MATH	mathematics
KITH	one's friend and neighbors	MESH	to entangle
KNISH	dough stuffed with filling and fried	MILCH	giving milk
		MIRTH	gaiety
KOPH	a Hebrew letter	MONTH	period of approximately 30 days
LAICH	laigh		
LAIGH	a lowland	MOOCH	to obtain without paying
LAITH	loath	MORPH	a type of phoneme
LAKH	sum of one hundred thousand	MOTH	a winged insect
		MOUCH	to mooch
LARCH	a coniferous tree	MOUTH	to put into the mouth
LASH	to strike with a whip	MUCH	a great amount
LATCH	a type of fastening device	MULCH	protective covering for the soil
LATH	thin strips of wood		
LAUGH	to express mirth by a series of inarticulate sounds	MUNCH	chew with a crackling sound
LEACH	to subject to the filtering action of a liquid	MUSH	travel over snow via dog sled
LEASH	restrain an animal with a line	MUSTH	a state of frenzy occurring in male elephants
LECH	letch	MUTCH	a close fitting cap
LEECH	to cling to and feed upon	MYNAH	myna
LETCH	a strong sexual craving	MYRRH	an aromatic gum resin
LOACH	a freshwater fish	MYTH	a type of traditional story
LOATH	unwilling	NEATH	beneath
LOCH	a lake	NEIGH	to utter the cry of a horse
LOTAH	small water vessel used in India	NIGH	near
		NINTH	one of nine equal parts
LOTH	loath	NOH	the classical drama of Japan
LOUGH	a lake		
LUNCH	to eat a noonday meal	NORTH	a point of the compass
LURCH	to sway	NOSH	to eat snacks between meals
LUSH	abounding in vegetation		
LYMPH	a body fluid containing white blood cells	NOTCH	to make an angular cut in
		NTH	pertaining to an indefinitely large ordinal number
LYNCH	to put to death without legal sanction		

NYMPH	a female spirit	PUNCH	perforate with a type of tool
OATH	a formal declaration or promise to fulfill a pledge	PUSH	to exert force to cause motion
OBEAH	a form of sorcery of African origin	QOPH	koph
OH	exclaim in surprise or desire	QUASH	to suppress completely
		QUOTH	said
OKEH	approval	QURSH	monetary unit of Saudi Arabia
OOH	to exclaim in amazement joy or surprise	RAH	to cheer on a team or player
OOMPH	spirited vigor		
OPAH	a marine fish	RAJAH	a king of prince in India
ORACH	a cultivated plant	RANCH	place for raising livestock
OUCH	a setting for a precious stone	RASH	acting without due caution
		RATCH	a ratchet
OUPH	ouphe – an elf or goblin	RATH	rathe
PAH	an exclamation of disgust	RAYAH	non-Muslim inhabitant of Turkey
PARCH	to make very dry		
PASH	to strike violently	REACH	to stretch out or put forth
PATCH	to mend or cover a hole	RESH	a Hebrew letter
PATH	a trodden way or track	RETCH	to make an effort to vomit
PEACH	to inform against someone	RICH	having wealth
PECH	to pant	ROACH	to cause to arch
PERCH	to sit on an elevated place	ROTCH	rotche – small aquatic bird
PINCH	to squeeze between two edges or surfaces	ROUGH	having an uneven surface
		ROUTH	an abundance
PISH	to express contempt	ROWTH	routh – abundance, plenty
PITCH	to throw	RUSH	to move swiftly
PITH	to sever the spinal cord of	RUTH	compassion
PLASH	to weave together	SANGH	an association promoting unity between different groups in Hinduism
PLUSH	luxurious		
POACH	to trespass for the purpose of taking game or fish		
		SASH	to furnish with a frame in which glass is set
POH	used to express disgust		
POOCH	a dog	SAUCH	saugh - sallow
POOH	to express contempt for	SAUGH	a willow tree
PORCH	a covered structure at the entrance to a building	SELAH	a word marking the end of a verse in the Psalms
POSH	stylish or elegant	SH	used to urge silence
POUCH	a small flexible receptacle	SHAH	an Iranian ruler
PSYCH	to put into the proper frame of mind	SHH	sh – used to urge silence
		SHUSH	to silence
PUGH	used to express disgust	SIGH	a deep audible breath
		SINH	a hyperbolic function

SITH	since	TILTH	tillage
SIXTH	one of six equal parts	TOOTH	one of the hard structures in a row on each jaw
SLASH	cut with sweeping strokes		
SLOSH	move with a splashing motion	TOPH	tufa
		TORAH	the body of Jewish law
SLOTH	slow moving arboreal mammal	TORCH	to set on fire
		TOSH	nonsense
SLUSH	partly melted snow	TOUCH	to come into contact with
SMASH	to shatter violently	TOUGH	strong & resilient
SMITH	a worker in metals	TRASH	worthless or waste matter
SNASH	abusive language	TROTH	to betroth
SNATH	the handle of a scythe	TRUTH	conformity to fact or reality
SOOTH	true	TUSH	to tusk
SOPH	a sophomore	UGH	the sound of a cough or grunt
SOTH	sooth		
SOUGH	a moaning or sighing sound	VETCH	a climbing plant
SOUTH	cardinal point of the compass	WASH	to cleanse by applying a liquid
STAPH	any of various spherical bacteria	WATCH	to observe carefully
		WAUGH	damp
STASH	to store in a secret place	WEIGH	to determine the weight of
STICH	a line of poetry	WELCH	to welsh
SUBAH	a province of India	WELSH	to fail to pay a debt
SUCH	of that kind	WENCH	to consort with prostitutes
SUGH	to sough	WHICH	what particular one or ones
SURAH	a silk fabric		
SWASH	to swagger	WHISH	to move with a hissing sound
SWATH	a row of cut grass or grain		
SWISH	to move with a prolonged hissing sound	WICH	wych
		WIDTH	extent from side to side
SWITH	quickly	WINCH	a hoisting machine
SYLPH	slender graceful girl or woman	WISH	to want to attain something
SYNCH	to sync	WITCH	to bewitch
TACH	a device for indicating speed	WITH	in the company of
		WOOSH	to whoosh
TEACH	to impart knowledge	WORTH	to befall
TEETH	of tooth	WRATH	to make wrathful
TENCH	a freshwater fish	WROTH	very angry
TENTH	one of ten equal parts	WYCH	a European elm
TETH	a Hebrew letter	YAH	exclamation of disgust
TEUCH	teugh	YEAH	yes
TEUGH	tough	YEH	yeah
THIGH	a part of the leg	YIRTH	yird - earth

U H

YODH	yod – a Hebrew letter
YOGH	a Middle English letter
YOUTH	a young person
ZILCH	nothing

I

AALII	a tropical tree
ABRI	a bomb shelter
ACARI	of acarus
AI	a three-toed sloth
AMI	a friend
ANI	a tropical bird
ANIMI	anime
ANTI	one that is opposed
ASCI	of ascus
ASSAI	a tropical tree
AUREI	of aureus
BANI	edits
BASSI	of basso
BENNI	benne
BI	a bisexual
BLINI	small pancake served with caviar
BOCCI	boccie
CADI	a Muslim judge
CAMPI	of campo
CARPI	of carpus
CEDI	a monetary unit of Ghana
CESTI	of cestus
CHI	a Greek letter
CHILI	a hot pepper
CIRRI	of cirrus
COATI	a tropical mammal
COCCI	bacterium
CONI	lower end of spinal cord
CORGI	a short-legged dog
CROCI	of crocus
CULTI	cults
DEFI	a challenge
DEI	used in names
DELI	a delicatessen
DHOTI	loincloth worn by Hindu men
DHUTI	dhoti

DISCI	of discus
DUCI	of duce
DUI	of duo
ELEMI	a fragrant resin
ELHI	school grades 1 through 12
ENNUI	a feeling of weariness
ENVOI	closing of poem or prose work
ETUI	case for holding small articles
FARCI	stuffed with finely chopped meat
FERMI	a unit of length
FUCI	olive brown seaweed
FUJI	a silk fabric
FUNGI	of fungus
GADDI	a hassock
GENII	of genius
GHAZI	a Muslim war hero
GHI	ghee
GYRI	a convolution of the brain
HADJI	one who has made a hadj
HAJI	hadji
HAJJI	hadji
HI	used as a greeting
HILI	marks or scars
HOURI	a beautiful maiden in Muslim belief
IMPI	a body of warriors
INDRI	a short-tailed lemur
ISSEI	a Japanese immigrant to the United States
JINNI	jinn
KADI	cadi
KAKI	a Japanese tree
KAMI	a sacred power or force
KANJI	a system of Japanese writing

KAURI	a timber tree	OKAPI	an African ruminant mammal
KEPI	a type of cap		
KHADI	khaddar	ORIBI	an African antelope
KHAKI	a durable cloth	PARDI	used as a mild oath
KHI	chi	PENNI	a Finnish coin
KIWI	a flightless bird	PERI	a supernatural being of Persian mythology
KRUBI	a tropical plant		
LANAI	a veranda	PETTI	petticoat
LATI	of lat	PHI	a Greek letter
LEi	a wreath of flowers	PI	a Greek letter
LI	a Chinese unit of distance	PILEI	of pileus
LIBRI	of liber	PILI	a Philippine tree
LICHI	litchi	POI	a Hawaiian food
LIMBI	of limbus	PRIMI	of primo
LOCI	of locus	PSI	a Greek letter
LUNGI	a loincloth worn by men in India	PULI	a long haired sheep dog
		PURI	poori
MAGI	of magus	QUAI	quay
MAQUI	maquis	QUASI	similar but not exactly the same
MAXI	a long skirt or coat		
MEDII	of medius	RABBI	a Jewish spiritual leader
MI	tone of the diatonic musical scale	RADII	of radius
		RAGI	an East Indian cereal grass
MIDI	a skirt or coat that extends to the middle of the calf	RAKI	a Turkish liqueur
		RAMI	of ramus
MINI	something distinctively smaller than others of its kind	RANI	the wife of a rajah
		RECTI	of rectus
		REI	erroneous English form for a former Portuguese coin
MIRI	of village commune		
MODI	of modus	RISHI	a Hindu sage
MOMI	faultfinders	SADI	sade
MUFTI	a judge who interprets Muslim religious law	SAKI	a Japanese liquor
		SALMI	a dish of roasted game bird
NAZI	a type of fascist	SARI	an outer garment worn by Hindu women
NIDI	of nidus - nest		
NISEI	one born in America of immigrant Japanese parents	SATI	suttee
		SEI	a rorqual
		SEMI	a freight trailer
NISI	not yet final	SENGI	a monetary unit of Zaire
NODI	of nodus – difficult situation	SENTI	a monetary unit of Tanzania
OBELI	marks to indicate doubtful words or paragraphs	SERAI	a Turkish palace
		SHOJI	paper partition or door in a Japanese house
OBI	obeah		

SHRI	on	YAGI	a type of shortwave antenna
SITI	of situs	YETI	the abominable snowman
SKI	long narrow strips of wood or metal	YOGI	a person who practices yoga
SOLDI	of soldo	YONI	a symbol for the vulva in Hindu religion
SOLI	of solo		
SORI	of sours	ZITI	a tubular pasta
SPAHI	a Turkish cavalryman	ZOMBI	a snake god voodoo cults in West Africa
SRI	used as a Hindu title of respect	ZORI	a type of sandal
STYLI	of stylus		
SWAMI	a Hindu religious teacher		
TALI	of talus		
TARSI	of tarsus		
TAXI	to travel in a taxicab		
TEMPI	of tempo		
TERAI	a sun hat with a wide brim		
THYMI	of thymus		
TI	tone of the diatonic musical scale		
TIKI	image of a Polynesian god		
TIPI	tepee		
TITI	an evergreen shrub or tree		
TOPI	a sun helmet		
TOPOI	of topos		
TORI	of torus		
TORII	gateway to a Japanese temple		
TORSI	of torso		
TRAGI	of tragus		
TSADI	sade		
TUI	a bird of New Zealand		
TUTTI	a musical passage performed by all the performers		
UNAI	unau		
UNCI	of uncus		
URAEI	of uraeus		
URARI	curare		
VAGI	of vagus		
WADI	the bed of a usually dry watercourse		
XI	a Greek letter		

J - END

AFLAJ	type of irrigation system
BENJ	an epic fail
FALAJ	type of irrigation system
HADJ	a pilgrimage to Mecca
HAJ	hadj
HAJJ	hadj
KILIJ	a type of saber
MUNJ	though Asiatic grass
RAJ	dominion sovereignty
TAJ	a tall conical cap worn in Muslim countries

J - ALL

AJAR	partly open	JAGGY	jagged
AJEE	agee	JAGRA	state of consciousness
AJIVA	inanimate matter	JAIL	a place of confinement
AJUGA	a type of ground cover plant	JAKE	all right; fine
BANJO	a musical instrument	JAKES	an outhouse
BIJOU	a jewel	JALAP	a Mexican plant
CAJON	a steep-sided canyon	JALOP	jalap
DJIN	jinni	JAM	to force together tightly
DJINN	jinni	JAMB	to jam
DOJO	school that teaches judo or karate	JAMBE	a jambeau
EJECT	to throw out forcibly	JAMMY	flukey, lucky
ENJOY	receive pleasure from	JANE	a girt or woman
FJELD	a high, barren plateau	JANTY	jaunty
FJORD	a narrow inlet of the sea between steep cliffs	JAPAN	to coat with a glossy lacquer
FUJI	a silk fabric	JAPE	to mock
GANJA	cannabis used for smoking	JAPER	one that japes
GANJE	person with ginger hair	JAR	to cause to shake
GADJO	an outsider in Romani culture	JARL	a Scandinavian nobleman
HADJ	a pilgrimage to Mecca	JATO	takeoff aided by jet propulsion
HADJI	one who has made a hadj	JATOS	plural jato
HAJ	hadj	JAUK	to dawdle
HAJI	hadji	JAUNT	to make a pleasure trip
HAJJ	hadj	JAUP	to splash
HAJJI	hadji	JAVA	coffee
JAB	to poke sharply	JAW	to jabber
JABOT	a decoration on a shirt	JAWAN	a soldier of India
JACAL	a hut	JAY	a corvine bird
JACK	raise with a type of lever	JAZZ	to enliven
JACKY	a sailor	JAZZY	lively
JADE	to weary	JEAN	a durable cotton fabric
JADED	cynical by experience	JEBEL	a mountain
JAG	to cut unevenly	JEE	to gee
JAGER	jaeger	JEEP	a type of motor vehicle
JAGG	to jag	JEER	to mock
		JEEZ	used as a mild oath
		JEFE	a chief

JEHAD	jihad	JINN	a supernatural being in Muslim mythology
JEHU	a fast driver		
JELL	to congeal	JINNI	jinn
JELLO	a gelatin dessert	JINX	to bring bad luck
JELLY	a soft semisolid substance	JIVE	to play jazz or swing music
JEMMY	to jimmy	JNANA	knowledge acquired through meditation
JENNY	a female donkey		
JERID	wooden javelin	JO	a sweetheart
JERK	move with a sudden motion	JOB	to work by the piece
		JOCK	an athletic supporter
JERKY	characterized by jerking movements	JOCKO	a monkey
		JOE	a fellow
JERRY	a German soldier	JOEY	a young kangaroo
JESS	to fasten straps around the legs of a hawk	JOHN	a toilet
		JOIN	to unite
JESSE	to jess	JOINT	to fit together by means of a junction
JEST	to joke		
JET	to spurt forth in a stream	JOIST	to support with horizontal beams
JETE	a ballet leap		
JETON	jetton	JOKE	to say something amusing
JETTY	to jut	JOKER	one that jokes
JEU	a game	JOLE	jowl
JEW	ethno religious group	JOLLY	cheerful
JEWEL	precious stones	JOLT	jar or shake roughly
JIB	to refuse to proceed further	JOLTY	marked by a jolting motion
		JORAM	jorum
JIBB	to shift from side to side while sailing	JORUM	a large drinking bowl
		JOSH	to tease
JIBE	to gibe	JOSS	a Chinese idol
JIBER	one that jibes	JOT	to write down quickly
JIFF	jiffy	JOTA	a Spanish dance
JIFFY	a short time	JOTTY	written down quickly
JIG	to bob	JOUAL	nonstandard dialects of Canadian French
JIHAD	a Muslim holy war		
JILL	a unit of liquid measure	JOUK	to dodge
JILT	to reject a lover	JOULE	a unit of energy
JIMMY	to pry open with a crowbar	JOUST	to engage in personal combat
JIMP	natty		
JIMPY	jimp	JOW	to toll
JIN	jinn	JOWAR	type of Old World grass
JINGO	a zealous patriot	JOWL	the fleshy part under the lower jaw
JINK	to move quickly out of the way		
		JOWLY	having prominent jowls
		JOY	to rejoice

JUBA	a lively dance	JUTTY	to jut
JUBE	a platform in a church	KANJI	a system of Japanese writing
JUDAS	a peephole		
JUDGE	to decide on critically	KOPJE	a small hill
JUDO	a form of jujitsu	MAJOR	to pursue a specific principal course of study
JUG	a large container with a narrow mouth and a handle		
		MOJO	magical charm bag
JUGA	freshwater snails	MUJIK	a Russian peasant
JUGAL	pertaining to the cheek or cheekbone	PUJAH	a form of ceremonial worship
JUGUM	a pair of the opposite leaflets of a pinnate leaf	PUNJI	a type of booby trapped stake
JUICE	the liquid part of a fruit or vegetable	RAJ	dominion sovereignty
		RAJA	rajah
JUICY	full of juice	RAJAH	a king of prince in India
JUJU	an object regarded as having magical power	SAJOU	a capuchin
		SHOJI	a paper partition or door in a Japanese house
JUKE	to fake out of position		
JULEP	a sweet drink	SLOJD	sloyd
JUMBO	a very large specimen of its kind	SOJA	the soybean
		TAJ	a tall conical cap worn in Muslim countries
JUMP	to spring off the ground		
JUMPY	nervous	THUJA	an evergreen tree or shrub
JUN	a coin of North Korea		
JUNCO	a small finch		
JUNK	to discard as trash		
JUNKY	worthless		
JUNTA	a political or governmental council		
JUNTO	a political faction		
JUPE	a woman's jacket		
JUPON	a tunic		
JURA	of jus		
JURAL	pertaining to law		
JURAT	a statement on an affidavit		
JUREL	a food fish		
JUROR	a member of a jury		
JURY	a group of persons sworn to render a verdict		
JUS	a legal right		
JUST	to joust		
JUT	to protrude		
JUTE	a strong coarse fiber		

K

ABACK	advance toward the back	BRINK	an extreme edge
ACOCK	cocked	BRISK	lively
ALACK	used to express sorrow or regret	BROCK	a badger
		BROOK	to tolerate
AMOK	a murderous frenzy	BRUSK	brusque
AMUCK	amok	BUCK	to leap forward and upward suddenly
APEAK	in a vertical position		
APEEK	apeak	BULK	into a mass
ARAK	arrack	BUNK	to go to bed
ARK	a large boat	BUSK	to prepare
ASK	to put a question to	CALK	to caulk
AUK	a diving seabird	CARK	to worry
BACK	to support	CASK	a strong barrel
BALK	to stop short and refuse to proceed	CAULK	to make watertight
		CHALK	a soft limestone
BANK	an institution dealing in money matters	CHARK	to char
		CHECK	to inspect
BARK	to cry like a dog	CHEEK	to speak impudently to
BASK	to lie in pleasant warmth	CHICK	a young bird
BATIK	a dyeing process	CHINK	to fill cracks fissures in
BAULK	balky	CHIRK	to make a shrill noise
BEAK	a bird's bill	CHOCK	to secure with a wedge of wood or metal
BECK	to beckon		
BILK	to cheat	CHUCK	to throw
BIRK	a birch tree	CHUNK	to make a dull explosive sound
BISK	bisque		
BLACK	being of the darkest color	CLACK	to make an abrupt, dry sound
BLANK	empty		
BLEAK	dreary	CLANK	to make a sharp, metallic sound
BLINK	the open and shut the eyes		
BLOCK	to obstruct	CLEEK	to clutch
BOCK	a dark beer	CLERK	an office worker
BOOK	to engage services	CUCK	to make a short, sharp sound
BOSK	a small wooded area		
BRANK	device used to restrain the tongue	CUNK	to make a soft, sharp, ringing sound
		CLOAK	to conceal
BREAK	to reduce to fragments	CLOCK	to time with a stopwatch
BRICK	to build with bricks		

CLONK	a dull thumping sound	FECK	value
CLUCK	to make the sound of a hen	FINK	to inform to the police
CLUNK	to thump	FLACK	a press agent
COCK	to tilt to one side	FLAK	antiaircraft fire
CONK	to hit on the head	FLANK	to be located at the side of
COOK	to prepare food by heating	FLASK	a narrow-necked container
CORK	to stop up	FLECK	tiny streaks or spots
CRACK	to break without dividing into parts	FLICK	to strike with a quick, light blow
CRANK	to start manually	FLOCK	to gather or move in a crowd
CREAK	to squeak		
CREEK	a watercourse smaller than a river	FLUNK	to fail an examination
		FOLK	a people or tribe
CRICK	to cause a spasm of the neck	FORK	a pronged implement
		FRANK	to mark (a piece of mail) for free delivery
CROAK	to utter a low hoarse sound		
		FREAK	to streak with color
CROCK	to stain or soil	FRISK	to move or leap about playfully
CROOK	to bend		
CUSK	a marine food fish	FROCK	to clothe in a long, loose outer garment
DAK	transportation by relays of men and horses		
		FUNK	to shrink back in fear
DANK	unpleasantly damp	GAWK	to stare stupidly
DARK	having little or no light	GECK	to mock
DAWK	dak	GEEK	a carnival performer
DECK	to adorn	GINK	a fellow
DESK	a writing table	GLEEK	to gibe
DHAK	an Asian tree	GOOK	goo
DICK	a detective	GOWK	a fool
DINK	to adorn	GREEK	something unintelligible
DIRK	to stab with a small knife	GUCK	a messy substance
DISK	to break up land with a type of farm equipment	GUNK	filthy sticky or greasy matter
DOCK	to bring into a wharf	HACEK	a mark placed over a letter to modify it
DRANK	past tense of drink		
DRECK	rubbish	HACK	to cut or chop roughly
DREK	dreck	HAIK	an outer garment worn by Arabs
DRINK	to swallow liquid		
DROUK	to drench	HANK	to fasten a Sail
DRUNK	intoxicated	HARK	to listen to
DUCK	to lower quickly	HAWK	to peddle
DUNK	to dip into liquid	HECK	hell
DUSK	to become dark	HICK	a rural person
ELK	a large deer	HOCK	to pawn

HOICK	to change directions abruptly	LARK	to behave playfully
HOLK	to hawk	LEAK	the escape of something through a breach or flaw
HONK	to emit a cry like that of a goose	LEEK	an herb used in cookery
HOOK	a bent piece of metal	LEK	a monetary unit of Albania
HOWK	to dig	LICK	to pass the tongue over the surface of
HUCK	a durable fabric	LINK	to connect
HULK	to appear impressively large	LOCK	to secure by means of a mechanical device
HUNK	a large piece	LOOK	to use one's eyes in seeing
HUSK	the outer covering	LUCK	to succeed by chance or good fortune
ILK	a class or kind	LUNK	a lunk head
INK	a colored fluid used for writing	LURK	to wait in concealment
IRK	to annoy or weary	MACK	mac
JACK	to raise with a type of lever	MARK	to make a visible impression
JAUK	to dawdle	MASK	covering to disguise the face
JERK	a sharp sudden motion	MEEK	lacking in spirit and courage
JINK	to move quickly out of the way	MERK	a former coin of Scotland
JOCK	an athletic supporter	MICK	an Irishman - offensive term
JOUK	to dodge	MILK	a whitish nutritious liquid
JUNK	to discard as trash	MINK	a carnivorous mammal
KAIAK	kayak	MIRK	murk
KAMIK	a type of boot	MOCK	to ridicule
KAPOK	a mass of silky fibers	MONK	a man who is a member of a secluded religious order
KAYAK	an Eskimo canoe	MOSK	mosque
KECK	to retch	MUCK	to fertilize with manure
KEEK	to peep	MUJIK	muzhik
KICK	to strike out with the foot or feet	MURK	dark
KINK	to form a tight curl or bend in	MUSK	a odorous substance secreted by certain animals
KIOSK	an open booth	NARK	to spy or inform
KIRK	a church	NECK	to kiss and caress in lovemaking
KNACK	to strike sharply	NICK	to make a shallow cut
KNOCK	to strike sharply	NOCK	to notch a bow or arrow
KOOK	an eccentric person	NOOK	a comer as in a room
KOPEK	kopeck	OAK	a hardwood tree or shrub
KULAK	a rich Russian peasant		
KYACK	a packsack		
LACK	to be without		
LANK	long and slender		

OINK	to utter the natural grunt of a hog	REEK	to give off a strong unpleasant odor
PACK	to put into a receptacle for transportation or storage	RICK	to pile hay in stacks
		RINK	a surface of ice for skating
PAIK	to beat or strike	RISK	expose to a chance of injury or loss
PARK	to leave a vehicle in a location for a time	ROCK	to move back and forth
PEAK	to reach a maximum	ROOK	to swindle
PECK	to strike with the beak or something pointed	RUCK	to wrinkle or crease
		RUSK	a sweetened biscuit
PEEK	to look furtively or quickly	SACK	a large bag
PERK	to carry oneself jauntily	SAMEK	a Hebrew letter
PICK	to select	SANK	past tense of sink
PINK	of a pale reddish hue	SARK	a shirt
PLACK	a former coin of Scotland	SCULK	to skulk
PLANK	long flat pieces of lumber	SEEK	to go in search of
PLINK	to shoot at random targets	SHACK	a shanty
PLONK	to plunk	SHANK	to hit sharply to the right
PLUCK	to pull out or off	SHARK	to live by trickery
PLUNK	to fall or drop heavily	SHEIK	an Arab chief
POCK	pustules caused by an eruptive disease	SHIRK	to avoid work or duty
		SHOCK	to strike with great surprise horror or disgust
PORK	the flesh of swine used as food	SHOOK	a set of parts for assembling a barrel or packing
PRANK	to adorn gaudily		
PRICK	to puncture slightly		
PRINK	to dress or adorn in a showy manner	SHUCK	to remove the husk or shell
		SICK	affected with disease
PUCK	a rubber disk used in ice hockey	SILK	a soft lustrous fabric
		SINK	to move to a lower level
PULIK	type of dog	SKINK	to pour out or serve as liquor
PUNK	dry decayed wood used as tinder		
		SKULK	to move about stealthily
QUACK	to utter the characteristic cry of a duck	SKUNK	to defeat overwhelmingly
		SLACK	not tight or taut
QUARK	a hypothetical atomic particle	SLANK	past tense of slink
		SLEEK	smooth and glossy
QUICK	acting with speed	SLICK	smooth and slippery
QUIRK	to twist	SLINK	to move stealthily
RACK	to place in a type of framework	SLUNK	past tense of slink
		SMACK	to strike sharply
RANK	to determine the relative position of	SMEEK	to smoke
		SMERK	to smirk
RECK	to be concerned about	SMIRK	to smile in a smug manner

68

SMOCK	a loose outer garment		TALUK	an estate in India
SNACK	to eat a light meal		TANK	a container usually for liquids
SNARK	an imaginary animal			
SNEAK	to move stealthily		TAROK	a card game
SNECK	a latch		TASK	to assign a job to
SNICK	to nick		TEAK	an East Indian tree
SNOOK	to sniff		THACK	to thatch
SNUCK	past tense of sneak		THANK	to express gratitude to
SOAK	to saturate thoroughly in liquid		THICK	a relatively great extent from one surface to its other
SOCK	a knitted or woven covering for the foot		THINK	to formulate in the mind
SPANK	to slap on the buttocks		TICK	to make a recurrent clicking sound
SPARK	small fiery particles	*TOCK*		
SPEAK	to utter words		TOOK	past tense of take
SPECK	to mark with small spots		TORSK	a marine food fish
SPICK	spic		TRACK	follow marks left by a person
SPIK	spic			
SPOOK	to scare		TRAIK	to trudge
SPUNK	to begin to bum		TREK	to make a slow or arduous journey
STACK	to pile			
STALK	to pursue stealthily		TRICK	to deceive
STANK	a pond		TROAK	to barter or trade
STARK	harsh in appearance		TROCK	a type of music
STEAK	a slice of meat		TRUCK	an automotive vehicle designed to carry loads
STEEK	to shut			
STICK	slender piece of wood		TRUNK	the main stem of a tree
STINK	to emit a foul odor		TSK	to utter an exclamation of annoyance
STIRK	a young cow			
STOCK	to keep for future sale or use		TUCK	to fold under
			TUPIK	an Eskimo tent
STOOK	to stack in a field for drying as bundles of grain		TUSK	long, pointed tooth extending outside of the mouth
STORK	a wading bird			
STUCK	past tense of stick		TWEAK	to pinch & twist sharply
STUNK	past tense of stink		UMIAK	an open Eskimo boat
SUCK	to draw in by establishing a partial vacuum		WACK	a wacky person
			WALK	to advance on foot
SULK	to be sulky		WARK	to endure pain
SWANK	imposingly elegant		WAUK	to wake
SWINK	to toil		WEAK	lacking strength
TACK	short sharp pointed nails		WEEK	a period of seven days
TALK	to communicate by speaking		WHACK	to strike sharply
			WHELK	a pustule

WHISK	to move quickly and easily
WICK	the loosely twisted fibers in a candle or oil lamp
WINK	to close and open one eye quickly
WOK	a cooking utensil
WORK	to exert one's powers of body for some purpose
WRACK	to wreck
WIREAK	to inflict
WRECK	to cause the ruin of
YACK	to yak
YAK	to chatter
YANK	to pull suddenly
YAPOK	small opossum
YELK	yolk
YERK	to beat vigorously
YEUK	to itch
YOLK	the yellow portion of an egg
YUK	to laugh loudly

L

AAL	an East Indian Shrub	AXIAL	pertaining to or forming an axis
ABOIL	boiling		
ACYL	univalent radical	AXIL	angle between upper side of a leaf and its supporting stem
AFOUL	entangled		
AHULL	abandoned and flooded		
AIL	to cause pain or discomfort to	BAAL	a false god
		BABEL	confusion
ALLYL	univalent radical	BABUL	a North African tree
AMPUL	ampule	BAGEL	a ring-shaped roll
AMYL	univalent radical	BAIL	transfer property temporarily
ANAL	pertaining to the anus		
ANGEL	a winged celestial being	BALL	a spherical object
ANIL	West Indian shrub	BANAL	ordinary
ANNAL	a record of a single year	BASAL	pertaining to the foundation
ANNUL	declare void or invalid		
ANVIL	a heavy iron block	BASIL	an aromatic herb
APPAL	to appall	BAWL	to cry loudly
ARGAL	therefore	BEDEL	an English university
ARGIL	a white clay	BEL	a unit of power
ARGOL	a crust deposited in wine cakes during aging	BELL	percussion instrument
		BERYL	a green mineral
ARIEL	an African gazelle	BETEL	a climbing plant
ARIL	outer covering of certain seeds	BEVEL	to cut an angle
		BEZEL	a slanted surface
ARTAL	unit of weight	BEZIL	bezel
ARTEL	a collective farm in Russia	BILL	a statement of costs
ARVAL	pertaining to plowed land	BINAL	twofold
ARYL	a univalent radical	BIRL	to rotate a floating-log
ATOLL	ring-shaped coral island	BOIL	to vaporize liquid
AURAL	pertaining to the ear	BOLL	to form pods
AVAIL	to be of use or advantage to	BOTEL	boatel
		BOWEL	to disembowel
AWFUL	extremely bad or unpleasant	BOWL	to play at bowling
		BRAIL	to haul in a sail
AWL	tool for making small holes	BRAWL	to fight
AWOL	absent without leave	BRILL	an edible flatfish
AXAL	to axial	BROIL	to cook by direct heat
AXEL	a jump in figure skating	BUBAL	a large antelope

BUHL	a style of furniture decoration
BULL	to push ahead
BURL	finish cloth by removing lumps
BUTYL	a hydrocarbon radical
CABAL	to conspire
CALL	to summon
CAMEL	a large, humped mammal
CANAL	an artificial waterway
CARL	a peasant
CAROL	a stately carriage
CAUL	a fetal membrane
CAVIL	to carp
CEIL	to furnish with a ceiling
CELL	to store in a honeycomb
CEORL	a freeman of low birth
CHIEL	a young man
CHILL	to make cold
CHURL	a rude person
CIBOL	a variety of onion
CIVIL	pertaining to citizens
COAL	to supply with coal
COIL	to wind in even rings
COL	a depression between two mountains
COMAL	smooth, flat griddle
COOL	moderately cold
COPAL	a resin
CORAL	mass of marine animal skeletons
COWL	to cover with a hood
CRAAL	to kraal
CRAWL	to move with the body on or near the ground
CRUEL	indifferent to pain of others
CULL	to select from others
CUPEL	to refine gold or silver in a cuplike vessel
CURL	to form into ringlets
CYMOL	cymene
DEAL	to trade or do business
DECAL	design transferred from specially prepared paper
DEDAL	daedal
DEIL	the devil
DEL	operator in differential calculus
DELL	a small wooded valley
DEVEL	to strike forcibly
DEVIL	to prepare food with pungent seasonings
DIAL	to manipulate a calibrated disk
DIEL	involving a full day
DILL	an annual herb
DIOL	a chemical compound
DIRL	to tremble
DOL	a unit of pain intensity
DOLL	to dress stylishly
DOMAL	an area of control
DOTAL	pertaining to a dowry
DOWEL	type of wooden pin
DRAIL	a heavy fishhook
DRAWL	speak slowly with vowels greatly prolonged
DRILL	to bore a hole in
DROLL	comical
DROOL	to drivel
DUAL	a linguistic form
DUCAL	pertaining to a duke
DUEL	to fight formally
DULL	mentally slow
DURAL	a brain membrane
DWELL	to reside
EARL	a British nobleman
EASEL	a three-legged frame
EEL	a snakelike fish
EGAL	equal
EL	an elevated railroad or train
ELL	the letter L
ENOL	a chemical compound
ENROL	to enroll
EQUAL	the same capability, quantity or effect

ERVIL	a European vetch	GAOL	to jail
ETHYL	a univalent chemical radical	GAVEL	to signal for attention by use of a gavel
EVIL	morally bad	GAYAL	a domesticated ox
EXCEL	to surpass others	GEL	to become like jelly
EXPEL	to force out	GHOUL	a demon
EXTOL	to praise highly	GHYLL	a ravine
FAIL	to be unsuccessful	GILL	type of net to catch fish
FALL	to descend under the force of gravity	GIMEL	a Hebrew letter
FARL	a thin oatmeal cake	GIRL	a female child
FATAL	causing death	GLIAL	pertaining to tissue of the central nervous system
FEAL	loyal	GNARL	to twist into a state of deformity
FECAL	pertaining to feces		
FEEL	to perceive through the sense of touch	GOAL	a point-scoring play in some games
FELL	to cause to fall	GORAL	a goat antelope
FERAL	wild	GRAAL	grail
FETAL	pertaining to a fetus	GRAIL	the cup used by Christ at the last supper
FIL	a coin of Iraq and Jordon		
FILL	to put in as much as can be held	GRILL	to broil on a gridiron
		GROWL	to utter a deep, harsh sound
FINAL	the last examination of academic course	GRUEL	to disable by hard work
FLAIL	to swing freely	GUL	a design in oriental carpets
FOAL	to give birth to a horse	GULL	to deceive
FOCAL	pertaining to a focus	GYRAL	gyratory
FOIL	to prevent the success of	HADAL	pertaining to deep parts of the ocean
FOOL	to deceive		
FOUL	offensive to the senses	HAIL	to welcome
FOWL	to hunt birds	HALL	a large room for assembly
FRAIL	fragile	HAMAL	a porter in eastern countries
FRILL	an ornamental ruffled edge		
FUEL	material used to produce energy	HARL	a hert
		HAUL	to pull with force
FUGAL	being in the style of a fungus	HAZEL	a shrub
		HEAL	to make sound or whole
FULL	filled completely	HEEL	the raised part of a shoe
FURL	to roll up	HEIL	to salute
FUSEL	an oily liquid	HELL	to behave raucously
FUSIL	a type of musket	HEMAL	pertaining to the blood
FUZIL	fusil	HERL	a feathered fishing lure
GAL	a girt	HEXYL	a hydrocarbon radical
GALL	to vex or irritate	HILL	a rounded elevation

HORAL	hourly	KRAAL	to pen in a type of enclosure
HOSEL	a part of a golf club		
HOTEL	a public lodging	KRILL	small marine crustaceans
HOVEL	a small miserable dwelling	LABEL	to describe or designate
HOWL	to cry like a dog	LALL	to articulate the letter r
HULL	remove the shell from a seed	LAPEL	extension of garment collar
		LEAL	loyal
HURL	to throw with great force	LEGAL	an authorized investment
IDEAL	a standard of perfection	LEVEL	to make even
IDOL	an object of worship	LIBEL	make a defamatory statement
IDYL	a literary work depicting scenes of rural simplicity		
		LOCAL	a train or bus making all stops
ILEAL	ileac		
ILIAL	iliac	LOLL	to lounge
ILL	an evil	LORAL	the space between the eye and bill of a bird
IMPEL	to force into action		
INDOL	heterocyclic organic compound	LOSEL	a worthless person
		LOYAL	faithful to one's allegiance
IODOL	an iodine compound	LULL	to cause to sleep or rest
JACAL	a hut	MAIL	to send by a governmental postal system
JAIL	a place of confinement		
JARL	a Scandinavian nobleman	MAILL	a payment
JEBEL	a mountain	MALL	to maul
JELL	to congeal	MARL	an earthy deposit containing lime clay and sand
JEWEL	precious stones		
JILL	a unit of liquid measure		
JOWL	the fleshy part under the lower jaw	MAUL	to injure by beating
		MEAL	food eaten in one sitting
JUGAL	pertaining to the cheek or cheekbone	MEDAL	a commemorative piece
		MEL	honey
JURAL	pertaining to law	MELL	to mix
JUREL	a food fish	MERL	merle
KAIL	kale	METAL	various ductile fusible and lustrous substances
KEEL	to capsize		
KEVEL	a belaying cleat or peg	MEWL	to whimper
KEVIL	kevet	MIAUL	to meow
KILL	to cause to die	MIL	a unit of length
KNEEL	to rest on the knees	MILL	to grind by mechanical means
KNELL	to sound a bell		
KNOLL	to knell	MODAL	pertaining to a mode
KNURL	to make grooves or ridges in	MODEL	to plan or form after a pattern
KOEL	an Australian bird	MOGUL	an important person
KOHL	a type of eye makeup		

MOHEL	a person who performs Jewish ritual circumcisions	OIL	liquid used for lubrication, fuel or illumination
MOIL	to work hard	OPAL	a mineral
MOL	mole	ORAL	an examination requiring spoken answers
MOLAL	pertaining to a mole		
MOLL	a gangster's girl friend	ORIEL	a type of projecting window
MOOL	soft soil		
MORAL	principles of right and wrong	OSMOL	a unit of osmotic
		OUSEL	ouzel
MOREL	an edible mushroom	OUZEL	a European bird
MOTEL	a roadside hotel	OVAL	egg shaped figure or object
MULL	to ponder	OWL	a nocturnal bird
MURAL	a painting applied directly to a wall or ceiling	PAIL	a watertight cylindrical container
NAIL	a slender piece of metal	PAL	to associate as friends
NASAL	sound uttered through nose	PALL	to become insipid
		PANEL	decorate with thin sheets of material
NATAL	pertaining to one's birth		
NAVAL	pertaining to ships	PAPAL	pertaining to the pope
NAVEL	a depression in the abdomen	PAROL	an utterance
		PAWL	a hinged mechanical part
NEROL	a fragrant alcohol	PEAL	to ring out
NEWEL	a staircase support	PEARL	smooth rounded masses formed in certain mollusks
NICOL	a type of prism		
NIDAL	pertaining to a nidus	PEDAL	operate with foot levers
NIHIL	nothing	PEEL	to strip off an outer covering
NIL	nothing		
NILL	to be unwilling	PENAL	pertaining to punishment
NIVAL	pertaining to snow	PERIL	to imperil
NODAL	of the nature of a node	PETAL	a leaf like part of corolla
NOEL	a Christmas carol	PHIAL	a vial
NOIL	a kind of short fiber	PIAL	membrane around brain
NOPAL	a cactus	PICAL	resembling a pica
NOTAL	pertaining to a notum	PICUL	an Asian unit of weight
NOVEL	a fictional prose narrative	PILL	small rounded masses of medicine
NULL	to reduce to nothing		
NURL	to knurl	PIPAL	a fig tree of India
OBOL	a coin of ancient Greece	POL	a politician
OCTAL	pertaining to a number system with a base of eight	POLL	to survey public opinion
		POOL	to combine in a common fund
OCTYL	a univalent radical		
ODYL	an od	PRILL	to convert into pellets
OFFAL	waste material	PROWL	to move about stealthily
		PUL	a coin of Afghanistan

PULL	to exert force to cause motion toward the force	SALOL	a chemical compound
		SAUL	soul
PUPIL	a student of a teacher	SCALL	a scaly eruption of the skin
PURL	to knit with a particular stitch	SCHUL	shul
		SCOWL	to frown angrily
QUAIL	to cower	SCULL	to propel with a type of oar
QUELL	to suppress	SEAL	to close or make secure against access leakage
QUILL	to press small ridges in		
RAIL	to scold in abusive or insolent language	SEEL	to stitch closed the eyes of as a falcon in training
RATAL	an amount on which rates are assessed	SEL	sell
		SEL	to give to another for money or other consideration
RATEL	a carnivorous mammal		
REAL	having actual existence		
REBEL	to oppose the established government of one's land	SEPAL	one of the individual leaves of a calyx
REEL	to wind on a type of rotary device	SERAL	pertaining to a series of ecological changes
REFEL	to reject	SHALL	to express futurity, inevitability or command
REGAL	of or befitting a king		
RENAL	pertaining to the kidneys	SHAUL	to shoal
REPEL	to drive back	SHAWL	a piece of cloth worn as a covering
REVEL	to engage in revelry		
RIAL	a monetary unit of Iran	SHIEL	shieling
RIEL	a monetary unit of Cambodia	SHELL	a hard outer covering
		SHEOL	hell
RILL	a small brook	SHEQEL	Israeli unit of currency
RIVAL	to strive to equal or surpass	SHIEL	shieling
		SHILL	to act as a decoy
RIYAL	a monetary unit of Saudi Arabia	SHOAL	shallow
		SHOOL	to shovel
ROIL	to make muddy	SHORL	schorl
ROLL	to move along by repeatedly turning over	SHUL	a synagogue
		SIAL	a type of rock formation
ROTL	a unit of weight in Muslim countries	SIBYL	a female prophet
		SIGIL	an official seal
ROWEL	to prick with a spiked wheel in order to urge forward	Sill	horizontal piece bearing the upright portion of a frame
ROYAL	a size of printing paper	SISAL	a strong fiber used for rope
RURAL	pertaining to the country	SKILL	ability to do something well
SAIL	to move by the action of wind		
		SKIRL	to produce a shrill sound
SAL	salt	SKOAL	to drink to the health of

SKULL	the framework of the head	TALL	having great height
SMALL	of limited size or quantity	TAMAL	tamale
SMELL	to perceive by olfactory nerves	TEAL	a river duck
		TELL	to give a detailed account of
SNAIL	to move slowly		
SNARL	to growl viciously	TEPAL	a division of a perianth
SNELL	a short line which attaches fishhook to a longer line	THILL	a shaft of a vehicle
		THIOL	a sulfur compound
SNOOL	to yield meekly	THIRL	to thrill
SOIL	to make dirty	THURL	the hip joint in cattle
SOL	the fifth tone of the diatonic musical scale	TICAL	a former Thai unit of weight
SOREL	sorrel	TIDAL	pertaining to the tides
SOTOL	a flowering plant	TIL	the sesame plant
SOUL	spiritual aspect of human beings	TILL	to plow
		TIRL	to make a vibrating sound
SPAIL	spale	TOIL	to work strenuously
SPALL	to break up into fragments	TOLL	a fixed charge for a service
SPEEL	to climb	TOIYL	a univalent chemical
SPEIL	to speel	TONAL	pertaining to tone
SPELL	name or write the letters in order	TOOL	an implement used in manual work
SPIEL	to talk at length	TOTAL	ascertain the entire amount
SPILL	to run out of a container		
SPOIL	to impair the value or quality	TOWEL	an absorbent cloth
		TRAIL	to drag along a surface
SPOOL	to wind on a small cylinder	TRAWL	to fish by dragging a net along the sea bottom
STALL	to stop the progress of		
STEAL	to take without permission	TRIAL	a judicial examination
STEEL	a tough iron alloy	TRILL	to sing or play with a vibrating effect
STILL	free from sound or motion		
STOOL	to defecate	TRIOL	a type of chemical compound
STULL	a supporting timber in a mine		
		TROLL	a dwarf or giant of Teutonic folklore
SURAL	pertaining to the calf of the leg		
		TRULL	a prostitute
SWALL	swale	TUBAL	pertaining to a tube
SWELL	to increase in size or volume	TWILL	to weave so as to produce a diagonal pattern
SWILL	to swig	TWIRL	to rotate rapidly
SWIRL	move with a whirling motion	TYPAL	typical
		UMBEL	a type of flower cluster
TAEL	a Chinese unit of weight	UNTIL	up to the time of
TAIL	a hindmost part	USUAL	something that is usual

VAGAL	a cranial nerve	YELL	to cry out loudly
VAIL	to lower	YILL	ale
VAKIL	vakeel	YODEL	to sing with a fluctuating
VEAL	meat from a calf		voice
VEIL	sheer fabric worn over face	YOKEL	a naive or gullible rustic
VENAL	open to bribery	YOWL	utter a loud, long,
VEXIL	vexillum		mournful cry
VIAL	a small container for	ZEAL	enthusiastic devotion
	liquids	ZONAL	pertaining to a zone
VIGIL	a period of watchfulness	ZORIL	a small African mammal
VILL	a village		
VINAL	a synthetic textile fiber		
VINYL	a type of plastic		
VIOL	a stringed instrument		
VIRAL	pertaining to or caused by		
	a virus		
VIRL	a metal ring put around a		
	shaft to prevent splitting		
VITAL	necessary to life		
VOCAL	a sound produced with		
	voice		
WAIL	to utter a long mournful		
	cry		
WALL	an upright structure built		
	to enclose an area		
WAUL	to cry like a cat		
WAWL	cry plaintively		
WEAL	a welt		
WEEL	well		
WELL	to rise to the surface and		
	flow forth		
WHEAL	a cereal grass		
WHEEL	circular frames designed to		
	turn on an axis		
WHIRL	to revolve rapidly		
WHORL	a circular arrangement of		
	similar parts		
WILL	to decide upon		
WOFUL	woeful		
WOOL	the dense soft hair of some		
	mammals		
XYLOL	xylene		
XYLYL	a univalent radical		
YAWL	to yowl		

M

ABEAM	at right angles to the keel of a ship
ABOHM	unit of electrical resistance
ABYSM	an abyss
ADEEM	to lake away
AHEM	used to attract attention
AIM	to direct toward a specified object or goal
ALARM	to frighten by a sudden revelation of danger
ALUM	a chemical compound
AM	1st person to be
ARM	to supply with weapons
ARUM	a flowering plant
ATOM	smallest unit of an element
AURUM	gold
AXIOM	a self-evident truth
BALM	a fragrant resin
BARM	the foam on malt liquors
BEAM	rays of light
BEDIM	to make dim
BEGUM	a Muslim lady of high rank
BERM	a ledge
BLOOM	to bear flowers
BOOM	a deep resonant sound
BOSOM	to embrace
BREAM	to clean a ship's bottom
BRIM	to fill to the top
BROOM	to sweep
BUM	to live idly
BUXOM	healthily plump
CALM	free from aggravation
CAM	a rotating piece of machinery
CAROM	to collide with and rebound
CECUM	body cavity with one opening
CELOM	coelom
CHAM	a khan
CHARM	to attract irresistibly
CHASM	a deep cleft in the earth
CHIRM	to chirp
CHUM	close friend
CLAIM	to demand as one's due
CLAM	bivalve mollusks
CORM	a stem of certain plants
CRAM	to fill or pack tightly
CREAM	a part of milk
CULM	to form a hollow stem
CUM	together with
CWM	a cirque
DAM	barrier to stop the water flow
DATUM	used as a basis for calculating
DEEM	to hold as an opinion
DEGUM	to free from gum
DEISM	a religious philosophy
DENIM	a durable fabric
DERM	derma
DIM	obscure
DOM	a title given to certain monks
DOOM	to destine to an unhappy fate
DORM	a dormitory
DRAM	to tipple
DREAM	images occurring during sleep
DRUM	a percussion instrument
DURUM	a kind of wheal
ELM	a deciduous tree
EM	the letter M
ENORM	enormous
ENYZM	enzyme
EXAM	an examination
FANUM	lanon

FARM	land devoted to agriculture	HILUM	small opening in a body organ
FILM	a thin layer or coating		
FILUM	anatomical structure	HIM	he
FIRM	unyielding to pressure	HOKUM	nonsense
FLAM	to deceive	HOLM	an island in a river
FLEAM	a surgical instrument	HUM	sing without opening the lips
FOAM	bubbly, gas and liquid mass		
FORAM	a marine rhizopod	IDEM	the same
FORM	to produce	IDIOM	expression peculiar to a language
FORUM	a public meeting place		
FROM	starting at	IHRAM	garb worn by Muslim pilgrims
GAM	to visit socially		
GAUM	to smear	ILEUM	a part of the small intestine
GEM	precious stones	ILIUM	a bone of the pelvis
GENOM	genome	IMAM	a Muslim priest
GERM	microorganism that causes disease	IMAUM	imam
		INARM	to encircle with the arms
GEUM	a perennial herb	ISM	a distinctive theory or doctrine
GLEAM	to shine with a soft radiance		
		ITEM	to itemize
GLIM	a light or lamp	JAM	to force together tightly
GLOAM	twilight	JORAM	jorum
GLOM	to steal	JORUM	a large drinking bowl
GLOOM	to become dark	JUGUM	opposite leaflets of a pinnate leaf
GLUM	being in low spirits		
GOLEM	a legendary creature	KALAM	a type of Muslim theology
GRAM	a unit of mass and weight	KILIM	an oriental tapestry
GRIM	stem and unrelenting	LAM	to flee hastily
GROOM	to clean and care for	LARUM	an alarm
GRUM	morose	LINUM	a plant of the flax family
GUM	a sticky viscid substance	LOAM	a type of soil
GYM	a room for athletic activities	LOCUM	a temporary substitute
		LOOM	appear in an enlarged and indistinct form
HAEM	heme		
HAKIM	a Muslim physician	LUM	a chimney
HALM	haulm	MADAM	woman manager of a brothel
HAM	to overact		
HAREM	section of a Muslim house reserved for women	MAIM	injure to cause lasting damage
HARM	to injure	MALM	a soft friable limestone
HAULM	a plant stem	MAXIM	brief statement of a general truth or principle
HELM	to steer a ship		
HEM	to provide with an edge	MEM	a Hebrew letter
HERM	a type of statue	MIASM	miasma

80

MIM	primly demure	QUALM	a feeling of doubt or misgiving
MINIM	a unit of liquid measure		
MOM	mother	RAM	to strike with great force
MUM	to act in a disguise	REALM	a kingdom
MUMM	to mum	REAM	to enlarge with a reamer
NEEM	an East Indian tree	REM	a quantity of ionizing radiation
NEUM	term in music theory		
NIM	to steal	RETEM	a desert shrub
NIZAM	a former sovereign of India	RHEUM	watery discharge from the eyes or nose
NOM	a name		
NORM	standard for specific group	RIM	an outer edge
NOTUM	part of the thorax of an insect	ROAM	move about without purpose
ODEUM	a theater or concert hall	ROOM	walled space within a building
ODUIM	hatred		
OGAM	ogham	RUM	an alcoholic liquor
OGHAM	an Old Irish alphabet	SAGUM	cloak worn by Roman soldiers
OHM	a unit of electrical resistance		
		SATEM	pertaining to a group of Indo-European languages
OLEUM	oil		
OM	mantra for contemplation of ultimate reality	SCAM	a swindle
		SCRAM	to leave quickly
ONIUM	characterized by a complex cation	SCRIM	a cotton fabric
		SCRUM	formation in rugby
OPIUM	an addictive narcotic	SCUM	impure or extraneous matter
OVUM	the female reproductive cell of animals		
		SEAM	line formed by sewing two pieces of fabric together
OXIM	a chemical compound		
PALM	to touch with the palm of hand	SEBUM	fatty matter secreted by glands of the skin
PAM	the jack of clubs in certain card games	SEDUM	a flowering plant
		SEEM	to give the impression of being
PERM	a long lasting hair setting		
PLASM	plasma	SEISM	an earthquake
PLUM	a neshy fruit	SERUM	watery portion of whole blood
POEM	a composition in verse		
PRAM	a flat bottomed boat	SHAM	to feign
PRIM	formally precise or proper	SHAWM	an early woodwind instrument
PRISM	a solid which disperses light into a spectrum		
		SHIM	a thin wedge
PROEM	an introductory statement	SIM	simulation
PROM	a formal dance	SKIM	to remove floating matter
PSALM	sacred songs	SLAM	to shut forcibly and noisily
		SLIM	slender

SLUM	squalid urban areas	VODUM	primitive religion of the West Indies
SMARM	trite sentimentality		
SOLUM	a soil layer	WARM	moderately hot
SPASM	abnormal involuntary muscular contraction	WHAM	forceful resounding blow
		WHELM	to cover with water
SPERM	a male gamete	WHIM	an impulsive idea
STEAM	water in the form of vapor	WHOM	objective case of who
STEM	ascending axes of a plant	WORM	small, limbless invertebrate
STORM	to blow violently		
STRUM	play instrument by running the fingers across strings	YAM	an edible root
		YOM	day
STUM	to increase the fermentation of by adding grape juice	ZIRAM	a chemical salt
		ZOOM	move with a humming sound
SUM	to add into one total		
SWAM	past tense of swim		
SWARM	to move in a large group		
SWIM	to propel oneself in water by natural means		
SWUM	past participle of swim		
TAM	a tight fitting Scottish cap		
TEAM	a group of persons associated in a joint action		
TEEM	to be full to overflowing		
TERM	to give a name to		
THARM	the belly		
THEM	the objective case of the pronoun they		
THERM	a unit of quantity of heat		
THRUM	to play a stringed instrument idly or monotonously		
TOM	the male of various animals		
TOOM	empty		
TOTEM	a natural object serving as the emblem of a family		
TRAM	to convey in a tramcar		
TRIM	neat & orderly		
UNARM	to disarm		
VELUM	a thin membranous covering		
VENOM	poisonous secretion of certain animals		
VIM	energy		

SPAM

N

ABOON	above	AVIAN	a bird
ACORN	fruit of the oak tree	AVION	an airplane
ACTIN	protein in muscle tissue	AWN	a bristle like appendage of certain grasses
ADMAN	man employed in the advertising business	AXMAN	one who wields an ax
ADORN	making attractive	AXION	hypothetical elementary particle
ADOWN	downward	AXON	central process of neuron
AEON	eon	AYIN	a Hebrew letter
AGAIN	once more	AZAN	a Muslim call to prayer
AGIN	against	AZON	a radio-controlled aerial bomb
AGON	conflict between main characters in Greek play	BACON	a side of a pig cured and smoked
AIN	belonging to	BAIRN	a child
AIRN	iron	BAN	to prohibit
AKIN	related by blood	BARN	a large storage building
ALAN	a large hunting dog	BARON	a lower member of nobility
ALOIN	laxative	BASIN	enclosed body of water
AMAIN	with full strength	BATON	a short rod
AMEN	word at end of prayer to express agreement	BEAN	to hit on the head
AMIN	amine	BEEN	past particle of be
AN	used before words beginning with a vowel	BEGAN	past tense of begin
ANCON	the elbow	BEGIN	to start
ANION	a negatively charged ion	BEGUN	past particle of begin
ANON	at another time	BEN	an inner room
APIAN	pertaining to bees	BETON	a type of concrete
APRON	garment worn to protect one's clothing	BIN	a large receptacle
ARGON	a gaseous element	BISON	an ox-like animal
ARPEN	measure of land	BLAIN	a blister
ARSON	fraudulent burning of property	BLIN	a blintze
ASHEN	consisting of ashes	BOGAN	a backwater or tributary
ASPEN	any of several poplars	BOON	a timely benefit
ATMAN	individual soul in Hinduism	BORN	having particular qualities from birth
AUXIN	substance used to regulate plant growth	BOSON	an atomic particle
		BOSUN	a boatswain
		BOURN	a stream

BRAIN	to hit on the head	COTAN	a trigonometric function
BRAN	the outer coat of cereals	COVEN	group of thirteen witches
BRAWN	muscular strength	COZEN	to deceive
BRIN	a rib of a fan	CROON	to sing softly
BROWN	of a dark color	CROWN	a royal headpiece
BRUIN	a bear	CUMIN	a plant used in cooking
BUN	small bread roll	CURN	grain
BUNN	bun	CUTIN	a waxy substance found on
BURIN	an engraving tool		plants
BURN	to destroy by fire	CYAN	a blue color
CABIN	a roughly built house	CYTON	the body of a nerve cell
CAIN	kain	DAMAN	a small mammal
CAIRN	a mound of stones set up	DAMN	to curse
	as a memorial	DARN	mend with interlacing
CAJON	a steep-sided canyon		stitches
CAN	a cylindrical container	DAVEN	to utter Jewish prayers
CANON	a law decreed by a church	DAWEN	past participle of daw
	council	DAWN	to begin to grow light in
CAPON	a gelded rooster		the morning
CARN	cairn	DEAN	the head of a faculty
CHAIN	series of connected rings	DEIGN	to lower oneself to do
CHIN	lower part of the face		something
CHON	a monetary unit of South	DEMON	an evil spirit
	Korea	DEN	to live in a lair
CHURN	stir briskly in order to make	DEVON	breed of small hardy cattle
	butter	DEWAN	an official in India
CION	a cutting from a plant	DIN	to make a loud noise
CLAN	united group of families	DIVAN	a sofa or couch
CLEAN	free from dirt or stain	DIWAN	dewan
CLON	a group of asexually	DIZEN	to dress in fine clothes
	derived organisms	DJIN	jinni
CODEN	a coding classification	DJINN	jinni
CODON	a triplet of nucleotides	DON	to put on
COGAN	a tall tropical grass	DOVEN	lazy, stale
COIGN	to quoin	DOWN	to cause to fall
COIN	metal currency	DOYEN	senior member of group
COLIN	the bobwhite	DOZEN	to stun
COLON	section large intestine	DRAIN	to draw off a liquid
CON	to study carefully	DRAWN	past participle of draw
CONIN	coniine	DROWN	to suffocate in water
CONN	direct steering of a ship	DUN	demand payment of a debt
COON	a raccoon	DURN	to damn
COPEN	a blue color	EARN	to gain or deserve for one's
CORN	to preserve with salt		labor or service

EBON	ebony	GAIN	to acquire
EIKON	a religious image	GAMIN	an urchin
ELAIN	olive oil	GAN	past tense of gin
ELAN	enthusiasm	GAUN	present participle of gae
ELFIN	an elf	GIN	to begin
ELOIN	to eloign	GIPON	jupon
EN	the letter N	GIRN	to snarl
ENFIN	finally	GIRON	gyron
EON	an indefinitely long period of time	GIVEN	something assigned as a basis for a calculation
EOSIN	a red eye	GLEAN	to gather little by little
ERN	erne	GLEN	a small valley
EVEN	flat and smooth	GOBAN	a board for a game
EYEN	of eye	GOON	a hired thug
FAGIN	a person who instructs others in crime	GOWAN	a daisy
		GOWN	long loose outer garment
FAIN	glad	GRAIN	form into small particles
FAN	device for putting air into motion	GREEN	color of growing foliage
		GRIN	to smile broadly
FANON	a cape worn by the pope	GROAN	to utter a low mournful sound
FAUN	a woodland deity of Roman mythology		
		GROIN	build with intersecting arches
FAWN	to seek notice or favor by servile demeanor		
		GROWN	mature
FEIGN	to pretend	GUAN	a large bird
FELON	a person who has committed a felony	GUN	a portable firearm
		GYRON	a heraldic design
FEN	a marsh	HAEN	past participle of hae
FERN	a flowerless vascular plant	HAVEN	to shelter
FICIN	an enzyme	HAZAN	a cantor
FIN	external paddle like structures	HEMIN	a chloride of heme
		HEN	a female chicken
FIRN	neve	HERN	a heron
FLAN	a type of custard	HERON	a wading bird
FLOWN	past participle of fly	HIN	a Hebrew unit of liquid measure
FOEHN	a warm, dry wind		
FOHN	type of wind	HISN	his
FOIN	thrust with pointed weapon	HOGAN	an Indian dwelling
		HONAN	a fine silk
FON	type of wind	HORN	a hard bonelike projection of the head
FROWN	to contract the brow in displeasure		
		HUMAN	a person
FUN	to act playfully	HUN	a barbarous destructive person
FURAN	a flammable liquid		

HWAN	a monetary unit of South Korea	KROON	a former monetary unit of Estonia
HYMEN	a vaginal membrane	LADEN	to lade
HYMN	a song of praise to god	LAGAN	goods thrown into sea with a buoy attached to enable recovery
HYSON	a Chinese tea		
ICON	a representation		
IKON	icon	LAIN	past participle of lie
IN	to harvest	LAPIN	a rabbit
INION	a part of the skull	LATEN	to become late
INN	a public lodging house	LAUAN	a Philippine timber
INURN	to put in an urn	LAWN	grass covered land
IODIN	iodine	LEAN	to deviate from a vertical position
ION	electrically charged atom		
IRON	a metallic element	LEARN	to gain knowledge by experience, instruction or study
JAPAN	a dark glossy lacquer		
JAWAN	a soldier of India		
JEAN	a durable cotton fabric	LEBEN	a type of liquid food
JETON	jetton	LEMAN	a lover
JIN	jinn	LEMON	a citrus fruit
JINN	a supernatural being in Muslim mythology	LEVIN	lightning
		LIEN	a legal right to hold or sell a debtor's property
JOHN	a toilet		
JOIN	to unite	LIGAN	lagan
JUN	a coin of North Korea	LIKEN	to represent as similar
JUPON	a tunic	LIMAN	a lagoon
KAIN	a tax paid in produce or livestock	LIMEN	a sensory threshold
		LIMN	depict by painting or drawing
KAON	a type of meson		
KARN	cairn	LIN	to yield
KEEN	enthusiastic	LINEN	fabric woven from flax fibers
KEN	to know		
KERN	to be formed with a projecting typeface	LININ	substance in nucleus of a cell
KHAN	an Asian ruler		
KILN	a type of oven	LINN	a waterfall
KIN	a group of persons of common ancestry	LION	a large carnivorous feline mammal
		LIPIN	a lipid
KININ	a hormone	LIVEN	to make lively
KIRN	to chum	LOAN	to lend
KNOWN	a mathematical quantity whose value is given	LODEN	a star used as a point of reference
KOAN	a paradox meditated on by Buddhist monks	LOGAN	a stone balanced to permit easy movement

LOIN	a part of the side between the ribs and the hipbone	NUMEN	a deity
LOON	a diving waterfowl	NUN	a woman belonging to a religious order
LORAN	type of navigational system	NYLON	a synthetic material
LORN	abandoned	OATEN	pertaining to oats
LOWN	peaceful	OCEAN	vast body of salt water
LUMEN	the inner passage of a tubular organ	ODEON	odeum
LUPIN	lupine	OFTEN	frequently
LYSIN	substance that can disintegrate blood cells or bacteria	OLDEN	pertaining to a bygone era
		OLEIN	liquid portion of a fat
		OMEN	a prophetic sign
MAIN	the principal part	ON	a side of the wicket in cricket
MAN	an adult human male		
MASON	to build with stone or brick	ONION	the edible bulb of a cultivated herb
MATIN	morning song as of birds		
MAUN	must	OPEN	affording unobstructed access, passage or view
MAVEN	trusted expert		
MAVIN	an expert	OPSIN	a type of protein
MEAN	to intend	ORCIN	crystalline substance
MELON	any of various gourds	ORGAN	a differentiated part of an organism
MEN	of man		
MESON	an atomic particle	ORPIN	yellow pigment
MIEN	demeanor	OVEN	enclosed heated compartment
MIZEN	mizzen		
MOAN	to utter a low mournful sound	RAVEN	type of large black bird
		OWN	to have as a belonging
MON	man	OXEN	plural of ox
MOON	to spend time idly	PAEAN	a song of joy
MORN	morning	PAEON	a metrical foot of four syllables
MORON	a mentally deficient person		
MOURN	express grief or sorrow	PAGAN	an irreligious person
MUCIN	a protein secreted by the mucous membranes	PAIN	suffering or distress
		PAN	to criticize harshly
MUN	man, fellow	PATEN	a plate
MUON	an atomic particle	PATIN	paten
NEON	a gaseous element	PAVAN	a slow stately dance
NINON	a sheer fabric	PAVIN	pavan
NITON	radon	PAWN	to give as security for something borrowed
NOMEN	the second name of an ancient Roman		
		PEAN	paean
NOON	midday	PECAN	a nut bearing tree
NOUN	a word used to denote the name of something	PEEN	beat with the non-flat end of a hammerhead
		PEIN	to peen

PEKAN	a carnivorous mammal	REIGN	exercise sovereign power
PEKIN	a silk fabric	REIN	to restrain
PELON	hairless	REMAN	to furnish with a fresh supply of men
PEN	instrument for writing		
PEON	an unskilled laborer	RENIN	an enzyme
PHON	a unit of loudness	RERAN	past tense of rerun
PIAN	a tropical disease	RERUN	present a repetition of a recorded performance
PIN	slender pointed piece of metal		
		RESIN	a viscous substance from certain plants
PINON	a pine tree		
PION	an atomic particle	RICIN	a poisonous protein
PIRN	a spinning wheel bobbin	RIN	to run or melt
PITON	a metal spike used in mountain climbing	RIPEN	to become ripe
		ROAN	animal coat sprinkled with white or gray
PLAIN	evident		
PLAN	a method for achieving an end	ROBIN	a songbird
		ROMAN	a metrical narrative of medieval France
POON	an East Indian tree		
PORN	pornography	ROSIN	to treat with rosin
PRAWN	edible shellfishes	ROUEN	breed of domestic ducks
PREEN	to smooth or clean with the beak or tongue	ROVEN	past participle of reeve
		ROWAN	a Eurasian tree
PUN	a play on words	ROWEN	a second growth of grass
PURIN	purine	RUIN	to destroy
PUTON	a hoax or deception	RUMEN	a part of the stomach of a ruminant
PYIN	a protein compound contained in pus		
		RUN	to move by rapid steps
PYLON	tall structure marking an entrance or approach	SABIN	unit of sound absorption
		SAIN	make Sign of the cross
PYRAN	a chemical compound	SALON	large room in which guests are received
QUEAN	a harlot		
QUEEN	a female monarch	SARIN	a toxic gas
QUERN	a hand turned grain mill	SASIN	an antelope of India
QUOIN	secure with type of wedge	SATIN	a smooth fabric
RACON	raccoon	SAVIN	an evergreen
RADON	a radioactive element	SAWN	past participle of saw
RAIN	water condensed from atmospheric vapor	SCAN	to examine closely
		SCION	a child or descendant
RAN	past tense of run	SCORN	to regard with contempt
RATAN	type of palm	SEDAN	a type of automobile
RAVIN	to raven	SEEN	past participle of see
RAYON	a synthetic fiber	SEMEN	fluid produced by male reproductive organ
RECON	a preliminary survey		
REDAN	a type of fortification	SEN	monetary unit of Japan

SERIN	a European finch	SUN	star around which the earth revolves
SETON	a type of surgical thread		
SEVEN	a number	SWAIN	a country boy
SEWAN	seawan	SWAN	to swear
SEWN	past participle of sew	SWOON	to faint
SHARN	cow dung	SWORN	past participle of swear
SHAWN	past participle of shaw	SWOUN	to swoon
SHEEN	to shine	SYN	syne
SHIN	climb by gripping and pulling with hands and legs	SYREN	siren
		TAIN	a thin plate
SHOON	plural of shoe	TAKIN	a goat like mammal
SHORN	past participle of shear	TALON	a claw of a bird of prey
SHOWN	past participle of show	TAN	convert hide into leather
SHUN	avoid	TARN	a small mountain lake
SIGN	to write one's name	TAXON	a unit of scientific classification
SIN	an offense against religious or moral law		
		TEEN	a teenager
SIREN	device producing a penetrating warning sound	TEN	a number
		TENON	a projection on the end of a piece of wood
SKEAN	a type of dagger		
SKEEN	skean	TERN	a seabird
SKEIN	wind into long loose coils	THAN	used to introduce the second element of a comparison
SKIN	membranous tissue covering body of animal		
SLAIN	past participle of slay	THEGN	thane
SOLAN	a gannet	THEIN	theine
SOLON	a wise lawgiver	THEN	that time
SON	a male child	THIN	having relatively little density or thickness
SOON	in the near future		
SORN	force oneself on others for food and lodging	THORN	a sharp rigid projection on a plant
SOWN	past participle of sow	TIGON	tiger lion hybrid
SOZIN	a type of protein	TIN	a metallic element
SPAWN	to deposit eggs	TITAN	a person of great size
SPEAN	to wean	TOKEN	to serve as a sign of
SPIN	draw and twist into threads	TOLAN	a chemical compound
SPOON	a type of eating utensil	TOMAN	a coin of Iran
SPUN	past tense of spin	TON	a unit of weight
SPURN	to reject with contempt	TOON	an East Indian tree
STAIN	to discolor or dirty	TORN	past tense of tear
STEIN	a beer mug	TOWN	a center of population smaller than a city
STERN	unyielding		
STUN	to render senseless or incapable of action	TOXIN	a poisonous substance
		TOYON	an evergreen shrub

TRAIN	instruct systematically	WHEN	the time in which something occurs
TUN	to store in a large cask		
TURN	move around a point	WHIN	furze
TWAIN	a set of two	WIDEN	to make wide or wider
TWEEN	between	WIGAN	a stiff fabric
TWIN	to bring together in close association	WIN	to be victorious
		WITAN	national council in Anglo-Saxon England
UHLAN	one of a body of Prussian cavalry		
		WITEN	of wit
ULAN	uhlan	WIZEN	to shrivel
UN	one	WOKEN	past participle of wake
UNION	persons united for a common purpose	WOMAN	an adult human female
		WOMEN	plural of woman
UNMAN	to deprive of courage	WON	to dwell
UNPEN	to release from confinement	WORN	affected by wear or use
		WOVEN	past participle of weave
UNPIN	to remove the pins	WREN	a small songbird
UPON	upon	WYNN	the rune for W
URBAN	pertaining to a city	XENON	a gaseous element
URN	a type of vase	XYLAN	a substance found in cell walls of plants
VAIN	filled with undue admiration for oneself	~~YAM~~	
		YAMEN	the residence of a Chinese public official
VAN	a large motor vehicle		
VEGAN	eats only plant products	YAMUN	yamen
VEIN	tubular blood vessels	YAPON	yaupon
VENIN	toxin in snake venom	YARN	to tell a long story
VIMEN	a long, flexible branch of a plant	YAWN	open the mouth wide with a deep inhalation
VIN	wine	YEAN	to bear young
VIXEN	a shrewish woman	YEARN	have deep desire
WAGON	a four-wheeled un-motorized vehicle	YEN	to yearn
		YIN	the feminine passive principle in Chinese cosmology
WAIN	a large open wagon		
WAKEN	to wake		
WAN	unnaturally pale	YOGIN	yogi
WARN	to make aware of impending danger	YON	yonder
		YOURN	yours
WAXEN	covered with wax	YUAN	a monetary unit of China
WEAN	end nourishment from mothers milk	YULAN	a Chinese tree
		YUPON	yaupon
WEEN	to suppose	ZAYIN	a Hebrew letter
WEN	benign tumor of the skin	ZEIN	a simple protein
WHEEN	a fairly large amount	ZOON	the whole product of one fertilized egg

O

ABMHO	unit of electrical conductance
ABO	an aborigine
ACHOO	ahchoo
ADO	bustling excitement
AERO	pertaining to aircraft
AGIO	premium paid to exchange currency
AGO	in the past
ALAMO	a softwood tree
ALSO	in addition
ALTHO	although
ALTO	low female singing voice
AMBO	a pulpit in early church
AMIDO	amide united with an acid radical
AMIGO	a friend
AMINO	amine with a nonacid radical
AMMO	ammunition
ARCO	direction to players of stringed instruments
ARVO	afternoon
AUDIO	sound reception
AUTO	a motor vehicle
AVISO	advice
AVO	a monetary unit of
AZO	containing nitrogen
BABOO	a Hindu gentleman
BANCO	bet in gambling game
BANJO	a musical instrument
BASSO	a low-pitched Singer
BEANO	a form of bingo
BILBO	a finely tempered sword
BINGO	a game of chance
BIO	a biography
BO	a pal

BOFFO	extremely successful
BOLO	a machete
BONGO	a small drum
BOO	to cry
BOYO	a boy
BOZO	a fellow
BRAVO	a hired killer
BRIO	liveliness
BROMO	a medicinal compound
BROO	a bree
BUBO	a welling of lymph gland
BUCKO	a bully
BUFFO	an operatic clown
BUNCO	to swindle
BUNKO	to bunco
BURRO	a small donkey
BUTEO	a hawk
CACAO	a tropical tree
CAMEO	portray in sharp, delicate relief
CAMPO	an open space in a town
CANSO	a love song
CANTO	division of a long poem
CAPO	pitch raising device for fretted instruments
CARGO	conveyed merchandise
CELLO	musical instrument
CENTO	literary work made of parts from other works
CERO	a large food fish
CHIAO	a monetary unit of China
CHICO	prickly shrub
CHINO	a strong fabric
CHIRO	a marine fish
CIAO	expression of greeting
CISCO	a freshwater fish
CLARO	a mild cigar

COCO	a tall palm tree	FADO	a Portuguese folk song
COHO	a small salmon	FANO	a fanon
COMBO	a small jazz band	FARO	a card game
COMPO	a mixed substance	FATSO	a fat person
CONGO	eel like amphibian	FICO	of little worth
CONTO	a Portuguese money of account *FINO*	FIDO	a defective coin
		FOLIO	to number the pages of
COO	sound of a dove	FORDO	to destroy
CREDO	a creed	FRO	away
CURIO	an unusual art object	FUGIO	a former coin of the United States
CUSSO	an Ethiopian tree		
CYANO	pertaining to cyanogen	FUNGO	fly ball hit to a fielder for practice in baseball
CYCLO	three-wheeled motor vehicle		
		GECKO	a small lizard
DADO	to set into a groove	GENRO	a group of elder
DAGO	an Italian or Spaniard a derogatory term	GESSO	a plaster mixture
		GIRO	an autogiro
DANIO	an aquarium fish	GISMO	a gadget
DATO	datto	GIZMO	gismo
DATTO	a Philippine tribal chief	GO	to move along
DEMO	a demonstration	GOBO	shield for microphone from extraneous sounds
DIAZO	containing a certain chemical group		
		GOGO	a discotheque
DIDO	a mischievous act	GOMBO	gumbo
DILDO	a penis substitute	GOO	sticky substance
DINGO	a wild dog of Australia	GREGO	a hooded coat
DISCO	a discotheque	GUACO	a tropical plant
DITTO	to repeat	GUTRO	a percussion instrument
DO	carry through to completion	GUMBO	the okra plant
		GUSTO	vigorous enjoyment
DODO	an extinct flightless bird	GYRO	a gyroscope
DOGGO	in hiding	HALLO	to shout
DOJO	school that teaches judo	HALO	to form a halo
DUO	an instrumental duet	HELIO	a signaling mirror
DUOMO	a cathedral	HELLO	to greet
DURO	a Spanish silver dollar	HERO	one who shows great courage
ECHO	repetition of sound by reflection of sound waves		
		HILLO	to hallo
EDOO	tropical plant	HIPPO	a hippopotamus
EGO	the conscious self	HO	used to express surprise
ERGO	therefore	HOBO	a vagrant or tramp
ERUGO	aerugo	HOLLO	to hallo
EURO	a large kangaroo	HOMO	a homosexual
EXPO	a public exhibition	HULLO	to hallo

HYDRO	electricity produced by waterpower	LINGO	incomprehensible language
		LINO	linoleum
HYPO	to inject with a hypodermic needle	LITHO	a type of print
		LLANO	an open grassy plain
IGLOO	an Eskimo dwelling	LO	used to attract attention or express surprise
IMAGO	an adult insect		
IMIDO	containing an imide	LOBO	the timber wolf
IMINO	containing an imine	LOCO	locoweed
INFO	information	LOGO	an identifying symbol
INTO	to the inside of	LOO	to subject to a forfeit
INTRO	an introduction	LOTTO	a game of chance
JATO	a takeoff aided by jet propulsion	MACHO	a person who exhibits machismo
JINGO	a zealous patriot	MACRO	type of computer instruction
JO	a sweetheart		
JOCKO	a monkey	MAKO	a large shark
JUDO	a form of jujitsu	MAMBO	a ballroom dance
JUMBO	very large specimen of its kind	MANGO	an edible tropical fruit
		MANO	stone for grinding foods
JUNCO	a small finch	MATZO	an unleavened bread
JUNTO	a political faction	MEMO	a note for something to be remembered
KAROO	karroo		
KAYO	to knock out	MENO	a musical direction
KAZOO	a toy musical instrument	METRO	a subway
KENDO	a Japanese sport	MEZZO	a female voice of a full deep quality
KENO	a game of chance		
KETO	pertaining to ketone	MHO	a unit of electrical conductance
KIDDO	form of familiar address		
KILO	a kilogram	MICRO	very small
KINO	a gum resin	MILO	a cereal grass
KOLO	a European folk dance	MISDO	to do wrongly
KOTO	a musical instrument	MISO	a type of food paste
KUDO	award; honor	MOLTO	a musical directions
KUSSO	cusso	MONDO	rapid question and answer technique used in Zen Buddhism
LAEVO	levo		
LARGO	slow musical movement		
LASSO	rope with a running noose	MONGO	a complete idiot
LENO	a style of weaving	MONO	an infectious disease
LENTO	slow musical movement	MOO	deep sound of a cow
LEVO	turning toward the left	MORRO	a rounded elevation
LIDO	fashionable beach resort	MOSSO	a musical direction
LIMBO	a condition of oblivion or neglect	MOTTO	short expression of a guiding principle
LIMO	a limousine	MOZO	a manual laborer

MUCRO	sharp point at end of certain plant and animal organs	PINTO	a spotted horse
		POCO	a musical direction
		POLIO	an infectious virus
MUNGO	a low quality wool	POLO	game played on horseback
NARCO	narc	PORNO	pornography
NEGRO	a member of the black race of mankind	POTTO	a lemur of tropical Africa
		PRAO	prau
NITRO	a nitrated product	PRIMO	main part in a musical piece
NO	a negative reply		
NOLO	a type of legal plea	PRO	argument in favor
NOO	now	PROSO	millet
OHO	expression of surprise	PUNTO	a hit or thrust in fencing
OLEO	margarine	RATIO	proportional relationship
OLIO	a miscellaneous	RATO	rocket assisted airplane
ONTO	to a position upon	RECTO	right hand page of book
ORDO	a calendar of religious directions	REDO	something done again
		REPRO	trail sheet for photo reproduction
ORTHO	reproduction in a photograph of the full range of colors in nature	RHINO	a rhinoceros
		RHO	a Greek letter
OTTO	attar – a fragrant oil	RODEO	exhibition of cowboy skills
OUTDO	exceed in performance	RONDO	a musical composition
OUTGO	to go beyond	ROTO	type of printing process
OUZO	a Greek liqueur	SAGO	a tropical tree
OVOLO	a convex molding	SALVO	discharge firearms simultaneously
PARGO	a food fish		
PASEO	a leisurely stroll	SAMBO	Latin American of mixed ancestry
PATIO	paved area adjoining a house		
		SCHMO	a stupid person
PEDRO	a card game	SCUDO	a former Italian coin
PENGO	a former monetary unit of Hungary	SECCO	art of painting on dry plaster
PEPO	a fruit having a fleshy interior and a hard rind	SEGNO	a musical sign
		SEGO	a perennial herb
PESO	monetary unit of some Spanish countries	SERVO	device used to control another mechanism
PETTO	the breast	SEXTO	sixmo
PHONO	a record player	SHAKO	a type of military hat
PHOTO	to photograph	SHMO	schmo
PIANO	a musical instrument	SHOO	to drive away
PINGO	a hill forced up by the effects of frost	SILO	tall cylindrical structure
		SIXMO	a paper size
PINKO	person who holds radical political views	SKIMO	an Eskimo
		SO	sol

PYRO

SOLDO	a former coin of Italy	VERSO	left-hand page of a book
SOLO	composition for single voice or instrument	VETO	to forbid or prevent
		VIDEO	television
SORGO	a variety of sorghum	VINO	wine
SPADO	castrated man or animal	VIREO	a small bird
STENO	a stenographer	WAHOO	a flowering shrub
SULFO	sulfonic	WHO	what or which person
SUMO	Japanese form of wrestling	WHOSO	whoever
SYBO	a spring onion	WILCO	indicates that a message will be complied with
TABOO	to exclude from use		
TACO	tortilla around a filling	WINO	one habitually drunk on wine
TANGO	a Latin-American dance		
TANTO	a musical direction	WO	woe
TAO	virtuous conduct	WOO	to seek the affection
TARDO	a musical direction	YAHOO	coarse, uncouth person
TARO	a tropical plant	ZERO	to aim at the exact center of a target
TEMPO	speed of a musical piece		
THIO	containing sulfur	ZOO	place where animals are kept for public exhibition
THO	though		
THORO	thorough		
THRO	through		
TIRO	tyro		
TO	in the direction of		
TONDO	a circular painting		
TOO	in addition		
TORO	a bull		
TORSO	trunk of a human body		
TOYO	smooth straw used in making hats		
TRIGO	wheat		
TRIO	a group of three		
TURBO	a turbine		
TWO	a number		
TYPO	a typographical error		
TYRO	a beginner		
UDO	a Japanese herb		
UMBO	the rounded elevation at the center of a shield		
UNCO	a stranger		
UNDO	to bring to ruin		
UNTO	to		
UPDO	an upswept hairdo		
UPO	upon		
UREDO	a skin irritation		

P

ABAMP	abampere	COMP	to play a jazz accompaniment
ALP	a high mountain		
AMP	ampere	COOP	to confine
ASP	a venomous snake	COP	to steal
ATOP	being on or at the top	COUP	to overturn
ATRIP	aweigh	CRAMP	to restrain or confine
BEBOP	a type of jazz	CRAP	to defecate usually considered vulgar
BECAP	to put on cap		
BEEP	to honk a horn	CREEP	to crawl
BLIMP	a non-rigid aircraft	CRIMP	to pleat
BLIP	to remove sound from a videotape	CRISP	brittle
		CROP	to cut off short
BLOOP	to hit a short fly ball	CROUP	a disease of the throat
BOP	hit or strike	CRUMP	to crunch
BUMP	to knock against	CUP	a small open container
BURP	to belch	CUSP	a pointed end
CAMP	of campo	CUTUP	a mischievous person
CAMP	to live in the open	DAMP	moist
CAP	a type of head covering	DAP	to dip lightly into water
CARP	find fault unreasonably	DEEP	extending far down from a surface
CHAMP	to chew noisily		
CHAP	split, crack, or redden	DIP	immerse briefly into a liquid
CHEAP	inexpensive		
CHEEP	to chirp	DORP	a village
CHIMP	a chimpanzee	DRIP	to fall in drops
CHIP	to break a small piece	DROOP	to hang downward
CHIRP	utter short, shrill sound	DROP	globules
CHOMP	to champ	DUMP	to let fall heavily
CHOP	sever with a sharp tool	DUP	to open
CHUMP	to munch	EQUIP	provide with whatever is needed
CLAMP	a securing device		
CLAP	strike one palm against the other	ESTOP	to impede by estoppel
		FLAP	to wave up and down
CLASP	to embrace tightly	FLIP	throw with brisk motion
CLIP	to trim by cutting	FLOP	to fall heavily and noisily
CLOMP	walk heavily and clumsily	FLUMP	to fall heavily
CLUMP	to form into a thick mass	FOP	to deceive
		FRAP	to bind firmly

CEP

96

FRUMP	a dowdy woman	KEEP	continue to possess
GALOP	a lively dance	KELP	a type of seaweed
GAMP	a large umbrella	KEMP	a champion
GAP	to make an opening in	KEP	to catch
GASP	to breathe convulsively	KIP	to sleep
GENIP	a tropical tree	KNAP	to strike sharply
GETUP	a costume	KNOP	a knob
GIMP	to limp	KNOSP	a knob
GIP	to gyp	KOP	hill
GLOP	a messy mass or mixture	LAMP	to look at
GOOP	a boor	LAP	to fold over something
GRAMP	grandfather	LEAP	to spring off the ground
GRASP	seize firmly with hand	LETUP	a lessening or relaxation
GRIP	to grasp	LIMP	to walk lamely
GROUP	an assemblage of persons or things	LIP	folds of flesh around the mouth
GRUMP	to complain	LISP	pronounce the letters s and z imperfectly
GULP	to swallow rapidly		
GYP	to swindle	LOOP	circular or oval openings
HAP	to happen	LOP	cut off branches or twigs
HARP	a type of stringed musical instrument	LOUP	to leap
		LUMP	shapeless masses
HASP	to fasten with a clasp	MAP	a representation of a region
HEAP	to pile up		
HELP	to give assistance to	MIXUP	a state of confusion
HEMP	a tall herb	MOP	an implement for cleaning floors
HEP	hip		
HIP	aware of most current styles and trends	MUMP	to beg
		NAP	to sleep briefly
HOLP	past tense of help	NEAP	a tide of lowest range
HOOP	a circular band of metal	NEEP	a turnip
HOP	to move by jumping	NETOP	friend; companion
HUMP	rounded protuberance	NIP	to pinch
HUP	a marching cadence	OP	a style of abstract art
HYP	hypochondria	ORLOP	the lowest deck of a ship
IMP	to graft feathers onto a bird's wing	OXLIP	a flowering plant
		PALP	appendage near mouth of invertebrate
JALAP	a Mexican plant		
JALOP	jalap	PAP	a soft food for infants
JAUP	to splash	PEEP	to utter a short shrill cry
JEEP	a type of motor vehicle	PEP	to fill with energy
JIMP	natty	PIMP	solicit clients for a prostitute
JULEP	a sweet drink		
JUMP	to spring off the ground		

PINUP	a picture that may be pinned up on a wall	SCOP	an Old English poet
PIP	to break through the shell of an egg	SCRAP	to discard
		SCRIP	a small piece of paper
PLOP	to drop or fall heavily	SCULP	to sculpt
PLUMP	well rounded and full	SCUP	a marine food fish
POLYP	an invertebrate	SEEP	to pass slowly through small openings
POMP	stately or splendid display		
POOP	to tire out	SETUP	the way something is arranged
POP	sharp explosive sound		
PREP	a preparatory school	SHARP	capable of cutting or piercing
PRIMP	dress or adorn carefully		
PROP	to keep from falling	SHEEP	a ruminant mammal
PULP	a soft moist mass of matter	SHIP	a vessel suitable for navigation in deep water
PUMP	device for moving fluids		
PUP	to give birth to puppies	SHOP	to examine goods with intent to buy
QUIP	to make witty remarks		
RAMP	to rise or stand on the hind legs	SIMP	a foolish person
		SIP	drink in small quantities
RAP	to strike sharply	SIRUP	syrup
RASP	rub with something rough	SKELP	to slap
REAP	to cut for harvest	SKEP	a beehive
REBOP	a type of music	SKIMP	to scrimp
RECAP	review by brief summary	SKIP	to move with light springing steps
REP	a type of virus		
REPP	rep	SLAP	strike with open hand
RIP	to tear or cut roughly	SLIP	to slide suddenly
ROMP	to play boisterously	SLOOP	a type of sailing vessel
ROUP	to auction	SLOP	to spill or splash
RUMP	the lower and back part of the trunk	SLUMP	to fall or sink suddenly
		SLURP	to eat or drink noisily
SALEP	starchy meal from roots of certain orchids	SNAP	make sharp cracking sound
		SNEAP	to chide
SALP	salpa	SNIP	cut with a short quick stroke
SAMP	coarsely ground com		
SAP	to deplete or weaken gradually	SNOOP	to pry about
		SOAP	a cleansing agent
SCALP	to remove an upper part	SOP	to dip or soak in a liquid
SCAMP	to perform in a hasty or careless manner	SOUP	to increase the power of
		STAMP	bring foot down heavily
SCARP	to cut or make into a steep slope	STEEP	inclined sharply
		STEP	move by lifting foot and setting it down in another place
SCAUP	a sea duck		
SCOOP	a spoon like utensil	STIRP	lineage

STOMP	to thread heavily	TWIRP	twerp
STOOP	to bend the body forward and down	TYPP	a unit of yam size
		UMP	to umpire
STOP	to discontinue progress	UNCAP	to remove the cap from
STOUP	a basin for holy water	UNRIP	to rip open
STOWP	stoup	UNZIP	to open the zipper of
STRAP	strip of flexible material	UP	to raise
STREP	spherical or oval bacteria	USURP	to seize & hold without legal authority
STRIP	remove outer covering		
STROP	to sharpen on a strip of leather	VAMP	to repair or patch
		VEEP	a vice president
STUMP	to baffle	WAP	to wrap
SUMP	low area serving as a drain for liquids	WARP	to twist or turn out of shape
SUNUP	sunrise	WASP	a stinging insect
SUP	to eat supper	WATAP	thread from roots of trees
SWAMP	to inundate	WEEP	to express sorrow by shedding tears
SWAP	to trade		
SWEEP	to clean with a brush	WHAP	to whop
SWOOP	make a sudden descent	WHAUP	a European bird
SWOP	to swap	WHELP	to give birth to
SYRUP	a thick sweet liquid	WHIP	instrument for administering punishment
TAMP	to pack down by tapping		
TAP	to strike gently	WHOMP	to defeat decisively
TARP	a protective canvas covering	WHOOP	to utter loud cries
		WHOP	to strike forcibly
THORP	a small village	WHUMP	to thump
THRIP	a British coin	WISP	small bunch or bundle
THUMP	a dull heavy sound	WOP	an Italian-an offensive term
TIP	to tilt	WRAP	wound or folded about
TOP	the highest part point	YAP	to bark shrilly
TRAMP	to walk with a firm heavy step	YAUP	to yawp
		YAWP	to utter a loud, harsh cry
TRAP	device for capturing animals	YELP	a sharp shrill cry
		YEP	yes
TRIP	to stumble	YIP	to yelp
TROMP	to tramp	YUP	yep
TROOP	to move or gather in crowds	ZAP	to kill or destroy
		ZIP	move with speed and vigor
TRUMP	to outdo		
TULIP	a flowering plant		
TUMP	tumpline		
TUP	to copulate with a ewe		
TWERP	a small impudent person		

WIMP

Q - End

CQ	code used by wireless operators
FAQ	list of questions and answers relating to a particular subject
IQ	measure of a person's intelligence
TALAQ	method of Sunni divorce
TRANQ	to be calm
UMIAQ	type of Eskimo boat

Q - ALL

AQUA	water	QUEAN	a harlot
EQUAL	same capability or effect	QUEEN	a female monarch
EQUIP	supply whatever needed	QUEER	deviating from normal
FAQIR	fakir	QUELL	to suppress
FIQUE	a tropical plant	QUERN	a hand turned grain mill
MAQUI	maquis	QUERY	to question
PIQUE	arouse anger or resentment	QUEST	to make a search
		QUEUE	to line up
QAID	caid	QUEY	a heiffer
QANAT	type of water management system	QUICK	acting with speed
		QUID	portion of something to be chewed
QAT	leaves of Catha edulis plant		
QINDAR	Albanian unit of currency	QUIET	making little or no noise
QOPH	koph	QUIFF	a forelock
QUA	in the capacity of	QUILL	to press small ridges in
QUACK	utter the cry of a duck	QUILT	stitch together with padding in between
QUAD	space out by quadrats		
QUAFF	to drink deeply	QUINT	a group of five
QUAG	a quagmire	QUIP	to make witty remarks
QUAI	quay	QUIPU	ancient calculating device
QUAIL	to cower	QUIRK	to twist
QUAKE	to shake or vibrate	QUIRT	to strike with a riding whip
QUAKY	tending to quake	QUIT	end one's occupation
QUALE	a property considered apart from things having the property	QUITE	to the fullest extent
		QUIZ	test knowledge
		QUOD	a prison
QUALM	feeling of misgiving	QUOIN	secure with a type of wedge
QUANT	propel through water with a pole		
		QUOIT	a throwing game
QUARE	queer	QUOTA	a proportional part or share
QUARK	hypothetical atomic particle		
		QUOTE	to repeat the words of
QUART	liquid measure of capacity	QUOTH	said
QUASH	to suppress completely	QURSH	monetary unit of Saudi Arabia
QUASI	similar but not exactly the same		
		SHEQEL	Israeli unit of currency
QUASS	kvass	SQUAB	a young pigeon
QUATE	quiet	SQUAD	small organized groups
QUAY	a wharf	SQUAT	to sit at one's heels

SQUAW	American Indian woman
SQUEG	to oscillate in an irregular manner
SQUIB	to lampoon
SQUID	ten armed mollusks
TOQUE	close fitting woman's hat
TRANQ	to be calm
TUQUE	a knitted wool cap
USQUE	usquebae

R

ABHOR	loathe	AUGUR	to foretell from omens
ABLER	comparative of able	AVER	to declare positively
ACTOR	a theatrical performer	BAKER	one that bakes
ADDER	venomous snake	BALER	one that bales
AFAR	a great distance	BAR	to exclude
AFTER	behind in place or order	BARER	comparative to bare
AGAR	substance obtained from certain seaweeds	BASER	comparative of base
		BAZAR	bazaar
AGER	one that ages	BEAR	to endure
AGGER	a mound of earth used as a fortification	BEER	an alcoholic beverage
		BEVOR	armor for the lower face
AIDER	one that aids	BIDER	one that bides
AIMER	one that aims	BIER	a coffin stand
AIR	mixture of gases surrounding the earth	BIKER	one that bikes
		BIRR	to make a whirring noise
AJAR	partly open	BITER	one that bites
ALAR	pertaining to wings	BLEAR	to dim
ALTAR	raised table used in worship	BLUER	comparative of blue
		BLUR	to make clear
ALTER	to make different	BOAR	make meals for a fixed price
AMBER	a fossil resin		
AMEER	amir	BOLAR	pertaining to bole
AMIR	muslim prince	BONER	a blunder
AMOUR	a love affair	BOOR	a rude person
ANEAR	to approach	BORER	one that bores
ANGER	to make angry	BOWER	to embower
APER	one that apes	BOXER	one that packs boxes
AR	the letter R	BOYAR	a former Russian aristocrat
ARBOR	a shady garden shelter	BRIAR	briar
ARDOR	intensity of emotion	BRIER	a thorny shrub
ARMER	one that arms	BUHR	a heavy stone
ARMOR	defensive body covering	BUR	to burr
ASKER	one that asks	BURR	a rough edge
ASPER	Turkish money of account	BUYER	one that buys
ASTER	a flowering plant	CABER	a heavy pole thrown as a trial of strength
ASTIR	moving about		
ATTAR	a fragrant oil	CANER	one that canes
AUGER	a tool for boring	CAPER	to frolic

Word	Definition	Word	Definition
CAR	an automobile	DEER	a ruminant mammal
CARER	one that cares	DEFER	to postpone
CATER	provide food and service	DEMUR	to object
CAVER	one that caves	DETER	to stop from proceeding
CEDAR	an evergreen tree	DICER	a device that dices food
CEDER	to assign or transfer	DIKER	one that dikes
CHAIR	to install in office	DIMER	molecule composed of two identical molecules
CHAR	to bum slightly		
CHARR	a small--scaled trout	DINAR	ancient Muslim coin
CHEER	to applaud with shouts of approval	DINER	one that dines
		DIRER	comparative of dire
CHIRR	a harsh, vibrant sound	DIVER	one that dives
CHOIR	to sing in unison	DOER	one that does something
CHURR	to make a vibrant sound	DOLOR	grief
CIDER	juice pressed from apples	DONOR	one that donates
CIGAR	roll of tobacco leaf for smoking	DOOR	a movable barrier for opening and closing an entranceway
CITER	one that cites		
CLEAR	clean and pure	DOPER	one that dopes
CODER	one that codes	DOR	a black European beetle
COIR	coconut husk fiber	DORR	dor
COLOR	visual attribute of objects	DOSER	one that doses
COMER	one showing great promise	DOTER	one that dotes
COOER	one that coos	DOUR	sullen
COPER	a horse dealer	DOWER	to provide with a dowry
CORER	utensil for coring apples	DOZER	one that dozes
COVER	to place something over	DREAR	dreary
COWER	to cringe	DRIER	one that dries
CRIER	one that cries	DRYER	drier
CRUOR	a blood clot	DUPER	one that dupes
·CUBER	device that cubes meat	DURR	durra
CUR	a mongrel dog	DYER	one that dyes
CURER	one that cures	EAGER	impatiently longing
CURR	to purr	EAR	the organ of hearing
CYDER	cider	EATER	one that eats
CYMAR	simar	EDGER	tool to trim a lawn's edge
CZAR	an emperor or king	EGER	eagre
DAMAR	dammer	EGGAR	egger
DARER	one that dares	EGGER	a kind of moth
DATER	one that dates	EIDER	a large sea duck
DEAIR	to remove air from	ELDER	an older person
DEAR	greatly loved	ELVER	a young eel
DEBAR	to exclude	EMBAR	to imprison
DECOR	style decoration		

EMBER	glowing fragment from a fire	FILER	one that files
EMEER	emir	FINER	comparative of fine
EMIR	an Arab chieftain	FIR	an evergreen tree
EMMER	a type of wheat	FIRER	one that fires
ENDER	one that ends something	FIVER	a five-dollar bill
ENTER	to come or go into	FIXER	one that fixes
EPHOR	a magistrate of ancient Greece	FLAIR	a natural aptitude
		FLEER	to deride
ER	used to express hesitation	FLIER	one that flies
ERR	to make a mistake	FLOOR	the level of a room
ERROR	mistake	FLOUR	ground meal of grain
ESCAR	esker	FLUOR	fluorite
ESKAR	esker	FLYER	flier
ESKER	ridge of gravel and sand	FOR	directed or sent to
ESTER	a chemical compound	FOUR	a number
ETHER	liquid anesthetic	FOYER	an entrance room or hall
EVER	at all times	FREER	one that frees
EWER	a large pitcher	FRIAR	member of religious order
EYER	one that eyes	FRIER	fryer
EYRIR	a monetary unit of Iceland	FRYER	one that fries
FACER	one that faces	FUMER	one that fumes
FADER	one that fades	FUR	a dressed animal pelt
FAIR	free from bias, dishonesty or injustice	FUROR	uproar
		GAGER	gauger
FAKER	one that fakes	GAMER	comp to game
FAKIR	a Hindu ascetic	GAPER	one that gapes
FAQIR	fakir	GAR	to cause or compel
FAR	at or to a great distance	GAUR	a wild ox
FARER	a traveler	GAZER	one that gazes
FAVOR	to regard with approval	GEAR	toothed machine parts
FEAR	to be afraid of	GIBER	one that gibes
FEMUR	a bone of the leg	GLAIR	to coal with egg white
FER	for	GLUER	one that glues
FETOR	an offensive odor	GNAR	to snarl
FEUAR	one granted land under Scottish feudal law	GNARR	to gnar
		GOER	one that goes
FEVER	abnormal elevation of the body temperature	GONER	one who is in a hopeless situation
		GOR	used as a mild oath
FIAR	type of absolute ownership of land	GUAR	drought tolerant legume
		GULAR	pertaining to the throat
FIBER	threadlike object	HAAR	a fog
FIFER	one that plays a fife	HAIR	a threadlike growth
FILAR	pertaining to a thread	HALER	a Czechoslovakian coin

HATER	one that hates	KEBAR	caber
HAVER	to hem and haw	KEFIR	a fermented beverage
HAYER	one that hays		made from cow's milk
HAZER	one that hazes	KEIR	kier
HEAR	to perceive by the ear	KIER	vat for dyeing fabrics
HEDER	a Jewish school	KITER	one that kites
HEIR	to Inherit	KNAR	a bump on a tree
HER	she	KNUR	a bump on a tree
HEWER	one that hewes	KOR	Hebrew unit of measure
HEXER	one that hexes	KYAR	coir
HIDER	one that hides	LABOR	to work
HIKER	one that hikes	LACER	one that laces
HILAR	pertaining to a hilum	LADER	one that lades
HIRER	one that hires	LAGER	to laager
HOAR	a white coating	LAIR	wild animal dwelling place
HOER	one that hoes	LAKER	a lake fish
HOMER	to hit a home run	LAMER	comparative to lame
HONER	one that hones	LAR	tutelary god in ancient
HONOR	to treat with respect		Roman household
HOPER	one that hopes	LASER	device that amplifies light
HOUR	a period of sixty minutes		waves
HOVER	hang suspended in air	LATER	comparative to late
HUGER	comparative of huge	LAVER	vessel for Hebrew
HUMOR	to indulge		ceremonial washings
ICIER	comparative of icy	LAYER	single thickness coating
ICKER	a head of grain	LAZAR	a beggar afflicted with a
IDLER	one that idles		loathsome disease
INCUR	to bring upon oneself	LEAR	learning
INFER	derive by reasoning	LEER	look with sideways glance
INNER	something that is within	LEGER	fishing bait made to lie on
INTER	to bury		the bottom
INVAR	a steel alloy	LEHR	a type of oven
ITHER	other	LEMUR	an arboreal mammal
IZAR	outer garment worn by	LEPER	one having leprosy
	Muslim women	LEVER	a rigid body used to lift
JAGER	jaeger		weight
JAPER	one that japes	LIAR	one that speaks falsely
JAR	to cause to shake	LIBER	a book of public records
JEER	to mock	LIDAR	electronic locating device
JIBER	one that jibes	LIER	one that lies or reclines
JOKER	one that jokes	LIFER	a prisoner serving a life
JUROR	a member of a jury		sentence
KABAR	caber	LIKER	one that likes
KAFIR	a cereal grass		

106

LINER	a commercial ship or airplane	MOLAR	a grinding tooth
LITER	a unit of capacity	MOOR	to secure a vessel by means of cables
LIVER	a secreting organ	MOPER	one that mopes
LOBAR	pertaining to a lobe	MOR	a forest humus
LONER	one that avoids others	MOTOR	to travel by automobile
LOPER	one that lopes	MOVER	one that moves
LOSER	one that loses	MOWER	one that mows
LOUR	to lower	MUCOR	a type of fungus
LOVER	one that loves another	MURR	murre
LOWER	to appear dark and threatening	MUSER	one that muses
		MUTER	comparative to mute
LUNAR	pertaining to the moon	NADIR	a point on the celestial sphere
LURER	one that lures		
MAAR	a volcanic crater	NAMER	one that names
MACER	official ceremonial staff	NAVAR	system of air navigation
MAIR	more	NEAR	within a short distance
MAJOR	to pursue a specific principal course of study	NEVER	at no time
		NITER	a chemical salt
MAKAR	a poet	NOIR	black
MAKER	one that makes	NOR	and not
MALAR	the cheekbone	NOTER	one that notes
MANOR	a landed estate	NUDER	comparative to nude
MAR	detract from perfection	OAR	long broad bladed poles
MASER	device for amplifying electrical impulses	OATER	a cowboy movie
		OCCUR	to take place
MATER	mother	OCHER	red or yellow iron ore used as a pigment
MAYOR	chief executive official of a city or borough		
		ODOR	property of a substance that affects the sense of smell
MAZER	a large drinking bowl		
METER	to measure by mechanical means		
		ODOUR	odor
MILER	one that runs a mile race	OFFER	to present for acceptance or rejection
MIMER	one that mimes		
MINER	one that mines	OGLER	one that ogles
MINOR	a specific subordinate course of study	OILER	one that oils
		OMBER	ombre
MIR	Russian peasant commune	OMER	a Hebrew unit of dry measure
MISER	one who hoards money greedily		
		OR	the heraldic color gold
MITER	raise to the rank of a bishop	ORDER	to give a command
		ORMER	an abalone
MIXER	one that mixes	OSIER	a European tree
MOHUR	a former coin of India		

OTHER	one that remains of two or more	POWER	to provide with means of propulsion
OTTAR	attar	PRIER	one that pries
OTTER	a carnivorous mammal	PRIOR	officer in a monastery
OUR	pronoun we	PRYER	prier
OUTER	a part of a target	PULER	one that pules
OVER	to the other side of	PUR	to purr
OWNER	one that owns	PURER	comparative to pure
OXTER	the armpit	PURR	low vibrant cat sound
OYER	a type of legal writ	QUEER	deviating from normal
PACER	horse whose gait is a pace	QINDAR	Albanian unit of currency
PAIR	to arrange in sets of two	RACER	one that races
PALER	comparative of pale	RADAR	an electronic locating device
PAPER	thin sheet made of cellulose pulp	RAKER	one that rakes
PAR	to shoot a standard number of strokes	RAPER	a rapist
		RARER	comparative to rare
PARER	one that pares	RASER	one that rases
PARR	a young salmon	RATER	one that rates
PATER	a father	RAVER	one that raves
PAVER	one that paves	RAZER	one that razes
PAWER	one that pawes	RAZOR	a sharp edged cutting instrument
PAYER	one that pays		
PAYOR	payer	REAR	one that rears
PEAR	a freshly fruit	RECUR	to happen again
PEER	to look searchingly	REFER	to direct to a source for information
PER	for each		
PETER	to diminish gradually	RICER	container perforated with small holes
PIER	structure from land out over water	RIDER	one that rides
PIKER	a stingy person	RIGOR	strictness or severity
PILAR	pertaining to hair	RIMER	one that rimes
PIPER	one that plays a tubular musical instrument	RIPER	comparative to ripe
		RISER	vertical part of stair step
PLIER	one that plies	RIVER	large stream of water
PLYER	plier	ROAR	a loud deep sound
POKER	one that pokes	ROGER	pirate flag with skull and crossbones
POLAR	straight line related to a point		
		ROPER	one that ropes
POLER	one that poles	ROTOR	rotating part of a machine
POOR	lacking means of support	ROVER	one that roves
POSER	one that poses	ROWER	one that rows
POUR	to cause to flow	RUER	one the rues
		RULER	one that rules

RUMOR	to spread by hearsay	SIZAR	student who receives financial assistance
SABER	a type of sword		
SABIR	a French based language	SIZER	sizar
SAFER	comparative of safe	SKIRR	to move rapidly
SAGER	comparative of sage	SLIER	comparative of sly
SAKER	a Eurasian falcon	SLUR	to pass over carelessly
SANER	comparative to sane	SMEAR	spread with sticky dirty greasy substance
SAPOR	flavor		
SATYR	a woodland deity of Greek mythology	SNEER	curl the lip in contempt
		SOAR	to fly at a great height
SAVER	one that saves	SOBER	having control of one's faculties
SAVOR	to taste with pleasure		
SAWER	one that saws	SOFAR	system for locating underwater explosions
SAYER	one that says		
SCAR	mark left by the healing of injured tissue	SOLAR	pertaining to the sun
		SONAR	underwater locating device
SCAUR	protruding isolated rock	SOPOR	abnormally deep sleep
SCOUR	to cleanse by scrubbing	SORER	superlative of sore
SEAR	to bum the surface of	SOUR	biting to the taste
SEDER	a Jewish dinner	SOWAR	mounted native soldier
SEER	a prophet	SOWER	one that sows
SENOR	a Spanish gentleman	SPAR	stout poles to support rigging
SER	a unit of weight of India		
SERER	comparative of sere	SPEAR	long pointed weapon
SEVER	to cut into parts	SPEER	to inquire
SEWAR	a medieval servant	SPEIR	to speer
SEWER	underground conduit for carrying off waste	SPIER	to speer
		SPOOR	to track
SHEAR	to cut the hair from	SPUR	a horseman's goad
SHEER	to deviate from a course	STAIR	used for going from one level to another
SHIER	horse with tendency to shy		
SHIRR	to draw into three or more parallel rows	STAR	a natural luminous body visible in the sky
SHOER	one that shoes horses	STEER	to direct the course of
SHYER	shier	STIR	pass an implement in circular motion
SIEUR	old French title of respect for a man		
		STOUR	dust
SIKER	secure	SUBER	phellem
SIMAR	a woman's light jacket	SUDOR	sweat
SIR	respectful form of address used to a man	SUER	one that sues
		SUGAR	a sweet carbohydrate
SITAR	a lute of India	SUPER	reinforce with a thin cotton mesh
SIVER	a sewer		
		SURER	comparative of sure

SWEAR	to utter a solemn oath	TWIER	tuyere
SWEER	lazy	TWYER	tuyere
TABER	to tabor	TZAR	czar
TABOR	to beat on a small drum	ULCER	a type of lesion
TAHR	a goat like mammal	UMBER	a brown pigment
TAKER	one that takes	UNBAR	to remove a bar from
TALAR	a long cloak	UNDER	in a lower position than
TALER	a former German coin	UPPER	shoe part above the sole
TAMER	one that tames	URGER	one that urges
TAPER	become gradually	USER	one that uses
	narrower at one end	USHER	to conduct to a place
TAPIR	a hoofed mammal	UTTER	an audible expression
TAR	a black viscous liquid	VAIR	fur for lining & trimming
TATER	a potato		medieval garments
TAWER	one that taws	VALOR	courage
TAXER	one that taxes	VAPOR	visible floating moisture
TEAR	liquid secreted by a gland	VEER	to change direction
	of the eye	VELAR	a kind of speech sound
THEIR	a possessive form of the	VEXER	one that vexes
	pronoun they	VICAR	a church official
THIR	these	VIER	one that vies
TIER	rows placed one above	VIGOR	active strength or force
	another	VIPER	a venomous snake
TIGER	a large feline mammal	VISOR	a projecting brim
TILER	one that tiles	VIZIR	vizier
TIMER	one that times	VIZOR	to visor
TITER	the strength of a chemical	WADER	one that wades
	solution	WAFER	to seal with an adhesive
TONER	one that tones		disk
TOPER	one that topes	WAGER	to risk on an uncertain
TOR	a high craggy hill		outcome
TORR	a unit of pressure	WAIR	to spend
TOTER	one that totes	WAKER	one that wakes
TOUR	travel place to place	WALER	Australian-bred horse
TOWER	to rise to a great height	WAR	state of armed conflict
TOYER	one that toys	WATER	transparent, odorless
TRIER	one that tries		tasteless liquid
TRUER	comparative of true	WAUR	worse
TSAR	czar	WAVER	move back and forth
TUBER	thick underground stem	WAXER	one that waxes
TUMOR	an abnormal swelling	WEAR	to have on one's person
TUNER	one that tunes	WEBER	a unit of magnetic flux
TUTOR	to instruct privately	WEER	comparative to wee
TUYER	tuyere – a nozzle	WHIR	a buzzing sound

110

WEIR	fence placed in a stream to catch fish
WHIRR	a buzzing sound
WHIRR	to whir
WIDER	comparative to wide
WIPER	one that wipes
WIRER	one that wires
WISER	comparative to wise
WIVER	winged creature with head of dragon
WOOER	one that woos
WRIER	past tense of wry
YAGER	jaeger
YAR	yare
YEAR	365 or 366 days
YIRR	to snarl
YOUR	belonging to you

S

ABYSS	a bottomless chasm
ADIOS	used to express farewell
AEDES	any of a genus of mosquitoes
AEGIS	protection
ALAS	express sorrow or regret
ALMS	money given to the poor
AMASS	to gather
AMISS	out of proper order
ANKUS	an elephant goad
ANUS	excretory opening of the alimentary canal
APHIS	an aphid
APSIS	sides in apse
ARCUS	an arch shaped cloud
ARGUS	an East Indian pheasant
ARLES	money to bind a bargain
ARRAS	a tapestry
ARRIS	ridge formed by the meeting of two surfaces
ARSIS	the unaccented part of a musical measure
AS	to the same degree
ASCUS	spore sac in fungi
ASPIS	aspic
ASS	a hoofed mammal
ATLAS	a male figure used as a supporting column
AURIS	the ear
AVENS	a perennial herb
AVGAS	gasoline for airplanes
AXIS	a straight line about which a body rotates
BALAS	a red variety of spinel
BANNS	a marriage notice
BASIS	foundation of something
BASS	an edible fish
BIAS	to prejudice

BIS	twice
BLESS	to sanctify
BLISS	happiness
BOGUS	not genuine, fake
BOLUS	a large pill
BONUS	an additional payment
BOSS	to supervise
BRASS	alloy of copper and zinc
BRAWS	fine clothes
BUS	large motor vehicle
BUSS	to kiss
CAMAS	camass
CESS	to tax or assess
CHAOS	a state of total disorder
CHESS	a two person board game
CLASS	to classify
CONUS	anatomical part in mammals
CORPS	a military rank
COS	a variety of lettuce
COSS	kos
CRASS	grossly vulgar or stupid
CRESS	a plant used in salads
CRIES	shed tears
CRIS	kris
CROSS	to intersect
CRUS	a part of the leg
CUSS	to curse
CUTES	of cutis
CUTIS	the corium
CYCAS	a tropical plant
DAIS	a raised platform
DEGAS	to remove gas from
DEMOS	people of an ancient Greek state
DES	used in names
DOES	present 3rd person of do

D 15
D 6 5

DOSS	sleep in any convenient place	GUESS	form an opinion with little or no evidence
DRESS	to put clothes on	GULES	the color red
DRIES	present 3rd person of dry	GYRUS	a ridge in the brain
DROSS	waste matter	HARDS	the coarse refuse of flax
EGADS	egad	HAS	present 3d person of have
EGIS	aegis	HERES	an heir
EIDOS	an essence	HILUS	hilum
ELVES	plural of elf	HIS	he
ENS	an entity	HISS	to make sibilant sound
EPOS	an epic poem	HOCUS	to deceive or cheat
EROS	sexual desire	HUMUS	decomposed organic matter
ERS	ervil		
ES	ess	HURDS	hards
ESS	the letter S	IBIS	a wading bird
ETHOS	the fundamental character of a culture	ICTUS	recurring beat in a poetical form
EYAS	a young hawk	IDES	a certain day in the ancient Roman calendar
FAVUS	a skin disease		
FECES	bodily waste	ILEUS	intestinal obstruction
FESS	to confess	INCUS	a bone in the middle ear
FETUS	unborn organism	IRIS	a part of the eye
FINIS	the end	IS	present 3rd person singular of be
FLOSS	a soft, light fiber		
FOCUS	point at which rays converge	IWIS	certainly, most likely
		JAKES	an outhouse
FOSS	fosse – ditch, moat	JESS	to fasten straps around the legs of a hawk
FRONS	anterior of insect's head		
FUCUS	brown algae	JOSS	a Chinese idol
FUSS	overly concerned with small details	JUDAS	a peephole
		JUS	a legal right
GAS	a substance capable of indefinite expansion	KAAS	kas
		KAS	a large cupboard
GAUSS	unit of magnetic induction	KISS	to touch with the lips
GENS	a type of clan	KOS	a land measure in India
GENUS	a kind sort or class	KOSS	kos
GIGAS	pertaining to variations in plant development	KRIS	a short sword
		KUMYS	fermented camel milk
GLANS	tip of penis or clitoris	KVAS	kvass
GLASS	a transparent substance	KVASS	a Russian beer
GLOSS	to make lustrous	LAPIS	a stone
GRASS	herbaceous plants	LARES	of lar
GROSS	flagrant	LASS	a young woman
		LENES	of lenis

LENIS	a speech sound	NARIS	a nostril
LENS	changes convergence of light rays	NATES	the buttocks
		NEGUS	an alcoholic beverage
LESS	not as great in quantity	NERTS	used to express defiance
LEWIS	a hoisting device	NESS	a headland
LIMES	a fortified boundary	NEVUS	a birthmark
LITAS	a former monetary unit of Lithuania	NEWS	report of recent events
		NEXUS	a connection or link
LIVES	of life	NIDUS	a nest or breeding place
LOCUS	a place	NISUS	an effort
LOESS	a soil deposit	NODUS	a difficulty
LOGOS	rational principle that governs the universe	NOUS	mind reason or intellect
		OASIS	green area in a desert
LORIS	an Asian lemur	OAVES	of oaf
LOSS	the act of one that loses	ONUS	burden or responsibility
LOTOS	lotus	OOPS	used to express mild apology or surprise
LOTUS	an aquatic plant		
LOUIS	a former gold coin of France	OPUS	a musical work
		ORNIS	avifauna
LUES	syphilis	ORRIS	a flowering plant
LUPUS	a skin disease	OS	an orifice or bone
LUSUS	an abnormality	OYES	oyez
LYSIS	disintegration of cells by membrane destruction	PARIS	a European herb
		PAS	a dance step
MAGUS	a magician	PASS	to go by
MANUS	the end of the forelimb in vertebrates	PAVIS	a large medieval shield
		PEDES	of peas
MASS	body of coherent matter	PENES	of penis
MAVIS	a songbird	PENIS	organ of copulation
MESS	to make dirty or untidy	PES	a foot or foot like part
METIS	person of mixed ancestry	PILUS	hair or hair like structure
MINUS	a negative quantity	PIOUS	religious reverence
MISS	fail to make contact	PISS	to urinate sometimes
MITIS	a type of wrought iron	PLUS	an additional quantity
MODUS	a mode	POLIS	ancient Greek city state
MOMUS	a carping person	PONS	nerve fibers in the brain
MONAS	a monad	PRESS	act with steady force
MONS	a protuberance of the body	PRISS	a prissy
MOSS	small leafy stemmed plants	PSOAS	a muscle of the loin
MUCUS	a viscid bodily fluid	PUBES	lower part of abdomen
MUSS	to mess	PUBIS	the forward portion of either of the hipbones
NABIS	a group of French artists		
NAOS	an ancient temple	PUS	fluid formed in infected tissue
NARES	of naris		

NU$ (handwritten)

114

PUSS	a cat	TOOTS	form of address to female
PYXIS	a pyxidium	TOPOS	a stock rhetorical theme
QUASS	kvass	TORUS	a large convex molding
RAMUS	a branch of a structure	TOSS	to throw lightly
RAS	an Ethiopian prince	TRANS	arrangement of atoms on
REBUS	a type of puzzle		sides of a molecule
REGES	of rex	TRASS	a volcanic rock
REIS	of real	TRESS	a long lock of hair
RES	a particular thing	TREWS	close fitting tartan trousers
RHUS	genus of shrubs or trees	TRIES	of try
RIBES	a flowering shrub	TROIS	the number three
RISUS	a grin or laugh	TRUSS	to secure tightly
RUBUS	plant of the rose family	TURPS	turpentine
SANS	without	UNCUS	a hook shaped anatomical
SASS	to talk impudently to		part
SEMIS	a coin of ancient Rome	UPAS	an Asian tree
SHIES	of shy	URUS	extinct European ox
SINUS	a cranial cavity	US	we
SIS	sister	VAGUS	a cranial nerve
SITUS	a position or location	VARUS	malformation of a bone
SOLUS	alone	VAS	an anatomical duct
SORUS	cluster of plant	VIBES	a percussion instrument
	reproductive bodies	VIRES	of vis
SPECS	eyeglasses	VIRUS	class of submicroscopic
STOSS	facing direction from which		pathogens
	a glacier moves	VIS	force or power
SUDS	to wash in soapy water	VOCES	of vox
SWISS	a cotton fabric	WAMUS	a heavy outer jacket
TABES	a syphilitic disease	WAS	past 1st singular of be
TALUS	a bone of the foot	WIS	to know
TAMIS	strainer made of cloth	WISS	to wish
	mesh	WIVES	plural of wife
TAPIS	material used for wall	WOOPS	oops
	hangings	WRIES	of wry
TASS	a drinking cup	XERUS	African ground squirrel
TAXUS	evergreen tree or shrub	YES	an affirmative reply
TELOS	an ultimate end	YIPES	yipe
TEXAS	the uppermost structure	YOURS	you
	on a steamboat	YWIS	certainly, most likely
THIS	the person or thing just	ZOOKS	used as a mild oath
	mentioned		
THUS	in this manner		
TONUS	normal state of tension in		
	muscle tissue		

T

ABAFT	advance toward stern
ABBOT	superior of a monastery
ABET	encourage and support
ABORT	to end prematurely
ABOUT	approximately
ABUT	to touch along a border
ACT	to do something
ADAPT	to make suitable
ADEPT	highly skilled
ADIT	entrance
ADMIT	allow to enter
ADOPT	take into one's family by legal means
ADULT	fully developed individual
ADUST	scorched
AFOOT	on foot
AFRIT	supernatural creature
AFT	toward the stem
AGENT	one authorized to act for another
AGIST	to feed and take care of for a fee, as livestock
AGLET	metal sheath end of lace
AIRT	to guide
AIT	a small island
ALANT	alan
ALLOT	to give as a share
ALOFT	in or into the air
ALT	high pitched musical note
AMBIT	external boundary
AMENT	mentally deficient person
AMORT	being without life
ANENT	in regard to
ANGST	a feeling of anxiety
ANT	a small insect
APART	not together
APORT	on the left side of a side
APT	suitable

ASSET (handwritten annotation)

ARGOT	a specialized vocabulary
ARHAT	a Buddhist who has attained nirvana
ARMET	a medieval helmet
ART	esthetically pleasing arrangement of parts
ASCOT	a broad neck scarf
AT	in the position of
ATILT	being in a tilted position
AUDIT	examine with to verify
AUGHT	a zero
AUNT	the sister of one's father or mother
AVAST	a command to stop
AVERT	to turn away
AWAIT	to wait for
BAHT	monetary unit of Thailand
BAIT	to lure
BAST	a woody fiber
BAT	to hit a baseball
BATT	a sheet of cotton
BEAST	an animal
BEAT	to strike repeatedly
BEAUT	something beautiful
BEET	a garden plant
BEFIT	to be suitable to
BEGET	to cause to exist
BEGOT	a past tense of beget
BELT	strap worn around waist
BENT	an inclination
BERET	a soft, flat cap
BESET	to assail
BESOT	to stupefy
BEST	to outdo
BET	to wager
BHOOT	bhut
BHUT	a small whirlwind
BIDET	basin used for washing

BIGHT	fasten with loop or rope	BUST	to burst
BIGOT	a prejudiced person	BUT	a flatfish
BINIT	a unit of computer information	BUTT	to hit with the head
		BUTUT	unit of Gambian currency
BINT	a woman	CADET	student at a military school
BIONT	a living organism	CANST	to tilt or slant
BIT	to restrain	CAPUT	a head or head like part
BITT	to secure a cable	CARAT	unit of weight for gems
BLAST	to use an explosive	CARET	a proofreader's symbol
BLAT	to bleat	CART	a two-wheeled vehicle
BLEAT	the cry of a sheep	CAST	to throw with force
BLENT	a past tense of blend	CAT	to hoist an anchor
BLEST	a past tense of bless	CELT	a primitive ax
BLET	a decay of fruit	CENT	100th part of a dollar
BLOAT	to swell	CHANT	to sing
BLOT	to spot or stain	CHAPT	a past tense of chap
BLUET	a meadow flower	CHART	to map out
BLUNT	not sharp or pointed	CHAT	to converse informally
BLURT	to speak abruptly	CHEAT	to defraud
BOART	bort	CHERT	a compact rock
BOAST	to brag	CHEST	a part of the body
BOAT	to travel by boat	CHIT	a short letter
BOLT	to sift	CHOTT	a saline lake
BOOST	to support	CIST	prehistoric stone coffin
BOOT	protective coverings for the feet	CIVET	a catlike mammal
		CLAST	a fragment of rock
BORT	a low-quality diamond	CLEAT	to strengthen with a strip of wood or iron
BOT	the larva of a botfly		
BOTT	bot	CLEFT	space made by cleavage
BOUT	a contest	CLIFT	cliff
BRACT	a leaf like plant part	CLIPT	a past participle of clip
BRANT	a wild goose	CLOOT	a cloven hoof
BRAT	a spoiled child	COACT	to act together
BRENT	brant	COAPT	fit together and make fast
BRIT	a young herring	COAST	to slide down a hill
BRITT	brit	COAT	an outer garment
BRUIT	to spread news of	COFT	past tense of coff
BRUNT	the main impact	COLT	a young male horse
BRUT	very dry	COMET	a celestial body
BUILT	a past tense of build	COMPT	to count
BUNT	to butt	COOPT	to elect or appoint
BURET	burette	COOT	an aquatic bird
BURNT	a past tense of burn	COSET	a mathematical subset
BURST	to break open suddenly	COST	a price for production

CLOT

117

COT	a light narrow bed	DINT	to dent
COUNT	to ascertain total units	DIPT	a past tense of dip
COURT	to woo	DIRT	earth or soil
COVET	to desire greatly	DIT	a dot in Morse code
CRAFT	to make by hand	DIVOT	a piece of turf
CREPT	past tense of creep	DIXIT	a statement
CREST	to reach a crest	DOAT	to dote
CROFT	a flowering plant	DOEST	a present 2nd person singular of do
CRUET	a glass bottle		
CRUST	an outer surface	DOIT	a former Dutch coin
CRYPT	a burial vault	DOLT	a stupid person
CUBIT	measure of length	DONUT	doughnut
CULET	a piece of armor for the lower back	DOST	a present 2d person singular of do
CULT	a religious society	DOT	tiny round mark
CURET	a surgical instrument	DOUBT	to be uncertain
CURST	a past tense of curse	DRAFT	conscript for service
CURT	abrupt	DRAT	to damn
CUT	to divide into parts with sharp edged instrument	OREST	past tenser of dress
		DRIFT	move along in a current
CYST	a sac	DRIPT	a past tense of drip
DAFT	insane	DROIT	a legal right
DART	to move suddenly	DROPT	excessive accumulation of serous fluid
DAUNT	to intimidate		
DAUT	to fondle	DUCAT	type of gold coins formerly used in Europe
DAVIT	a hoisting device		
DAWT	to daut	DUCT	a tubular passage
DEALT	a business transaction	DUET	musical composition for two
DEBIT	to charge with a debt		
DEBT	something that is owed	DUIT	dolt
DEBUT	a first public appearance	DUNT	strike with a heavy blow
DEFAT	to remove fat from	DURST	a past tense of dare
DEFT	skillful	DUST	minute particles of matter
DEIST	an adherent of deism	DWELT	a past tense of dwell
DELFT	an earthenware	EAST	cardinal point of the compass
DEMIT	to resign		
DENT	make a depression in	EAT	to consume food
DEPOT	a railroad or bus station	EBBET	a common green newt
DERAT	to rid of rats	ECLAT	brilliance
DICOT	plant with two seed leaves	EDICT	order having the force of law
DIDST	a past tense of do		
DIET	regulate sustenance	EDIT	prepare for publication
DIGHT	to adorn	EDUCT	something educed
DIGIT	a finger or toe	EFT	a newt

CRIT

EGEST	discharge from the body	FILET	to fillet
EGRET	a wading bird	FIRST	something that precedes
EIGHT	a number		all others
EJECT	to throw out forcibly	FIST	the hand closed tightly
ELECT	to select by vote	FIT	healthy
EMIT	send forth	FIXT	past tense of fix
EMMET	an ant	FLAT	having a smooth surface
ENACT	to make into a law	FLEET	swift
EPACT	difference of lengths of	FLINT	a spark-producing rock
	solar and lunar years	FLIRT	behave amorously without
ERECT	to build		serious intent
ERGOT	a fungus	FLIT	to move lightly
ERST	formerly	FLOAT	remain on the surface of a
ERUCT	to belch		liquid
ERUPT	to burst forth	FLOUT	to treat with contempt
ESCOT	to provide support for	FLUYT	a type of ship
ET	a past tense of eat	FOIST	to force upon slyly
EVENT	something that occurs	FONT	a receptacle for water used
EVERT	to turn outward		in baptism
EVICT	to expel by legal process	FOOT	terminal part of leg on
EXACT	precise		which the body stands
EXALT	to raise	FORT	a fortified enclosure
EXERT	to put into action	FOUNT	a fountain
EXIST	to be	FRAT	a college fraternity
EXIT	to go out	FRET	to worry
EXULT	to rejoice greatly	FRIT	fuse into a vitreous
FACET	a small plane surface		substance
FACT	known with certainty	FRITT	to frit
FAGOT	bind together in bundle	FRONT	a forward part
FAINT	to lose consciousness	FROST	deposit of ice crystals
FART	expel gas through anus	FRUIT	usually edible bodies of a
FAST	moving quickly		seed plant
FAT	an abundance of flesh	FUMET	odor of cooking meat
FAULT	to criticize	GAIT	move in a particular way
FEAST	to eat sumptuously	GAMUT	an entire range
FEAT	a notable achievement	GAST	to scare
FEET	of foot	GAT	a pistol
FEINT	deceptive movement	GAULT	a heavy thick clay soil
FEIST	dog of mixed breed	GAUNT	emaciated
FELT	to mat together	GAVOT	a French dance
FET	to fetch	GEEST	old alluvial matter
FIAT	an authoritative order	GELT	money
FIGHT	to attempt to defeat an	GEMOT	a public meeting in Anglo-
	adversary		Saxon England

GENET	a carnivorous mammal	GUILT	the fact of having committed an offense
GENT	a gentleman	GUST	sudden blasts of wind
GEST	a feat	GUT	intestines
GET	to obtain or acquire	GUYOT	a flat-topped seamount
GHAST	ghastly	HABIT	to clothe or dress
GHAT	a passage leading down to a river	HAET	a small amount
GHAUT	ghat	HAFT	to supply with a handle
GHOST	to haunt	HALT	to stop
GIANT	a person great size	HANT	to haunt
GIFT	something given	HART	a male deer
GIGOT	a leg of lamb	HAST	present 2d person singular of have
GILT	a gold coating	HAT	a covering for the head
GIRT	to gird	HAUNT	to visit frequently
GIST	main point of a matter	HEART	to hearten
GIT	an order of dismissal	HEAT	to make hot
GLEET	to discharge mucus from the urethra	HEFT	to lift up
GLINT	to glitter	HEIST	to steal
GLOAT	to regard with excessive satisfaction	HELOT	a slave or serf
		HENT	to grasp
GLOST	pottery coated with a glassy surface	HEST	a command
		HET	past tense of heat
GLOUT	to pout or look sullen	HIGHT	to command
GLUT	to feed or fill to excess	HILT	a handle for a weapon
GNAT	a small winged insect	HINT	to suggest indirectly
GOAT	a homed mammal	HIST	to hoist
GOT	past tense of get	HIT	to strike forcibly
GOUT	a metabolic disease	HOIST	to haul up mechanically
GRAFT	unite with a growing plant by insertion	HOLT	a grove
		HOOT	to cry like an owl
GRANT	to bestow upon	HORST	portion of earth's crust
GRAT	to weep	HOST	to entertain socially
GREAT	large or distinguished	HOT	a high temperature
GREET	address in a friendly way	HUNT	pursue for food or sport
GRIFT	to swindle	HURT	to injure
GRIPT	a past tense of grip	HUT	a simple shelter
GRIST	grain for grinding	IDIOT	mentally deficient person
GRIT	press the teeth together	INAPT	not apt
GROAT	an old English coin	INEPT	not suitable
GROT	a grotto	INERT	lacks active properties
GROUT	to fill with a thin mortar	INGOT	shape into a convenient form for storage
GRUNT	a deep guttural sound		
GUEST	to appear as a visitor	INLET	to insert

INPUT	enter data into computer	LAT	former monetary unit of Latvia
INSET	to insert		
ISLET	a small island	LEANT	a past tense of lean
IT	3d person singular neuter pronoun	LEAPT	past tense of leap
		LEAST	smallest in size
JABOT	a decoration on a shirt	LEET	a former English court for petty offenses
JAUNT	a pleasure trip		
JEST	to joke	LEFT	side of a body to the north when facing east
JET	spurt forth in a stream		
JILT	to reject a lover	LEGIT	legitimate drama
JOINT	to fix together by means of a junction	LENT	past tense of lend
		LEST	for fear that
JOIST	support with horizontal beams	LET	to hinder
		LICIT	lawful
JOLT	jar or shake roughly	LIFT	move to higher position
JOT	to write down quickly	LIGHT	having little weight
JOUST	engage in personal combat	LIGHT	to light
JURAT	statement on an affidavit	LILT	to sing rhythmically
JUST	to joust	LIMIT	to restrict
JUT	to protrude	LINT	accumulation of bits of fiber
KAPUT	ruined		
KARAT	a unit of quality for gold	LIST	to write down in a particular order
KARST	a limestone region		
KART	a small motor vehicle	LIT	past tense of light
KAT	an evergreen shrub	LOFT	an upper room
KEET	a young guinea fowl	LOOT	to plunder
KEMPT	neatly kept	LOST	not to be found
KENT	past tense of ken	LOT	to distribute proportionately
KEPT	past tense of keep		
KHAT	kat	LOUT	to bow in respect
KILT	make creases or pleats	LUNET	lunette
KIST	a chest box or coffin	LUNT	to emit smoke
KIT	to equip	LUST	an intense desire
KNELT	past tense of kneel	LYART	lyard
KNIT	to make a fabric by joining loops of yarn	MAGOT	a tailless ape
		MAIST	most
KNOT	a closed loop	MALT	germinated grain
KNOUT	flog with a leather whip	MART	to market
KRAFT	a strong paper	MAST	long pole on ship that supports rigging
KRAIT	a venomous snake		
KRAUT	sauerkraut	MAT	a dense mass
KYAT	monetary unit of Burma	MATT	to matte
LAST	to continue in existence	MAUT	malt

MAYST	present 2d person singular of may	NOWT	naught
		NUT	a hard shelled dry fruit
MEANT	past tense of mean	OAST	a type of kiln
MEAT	animal flesh used as food	OAT	a cereal grass
MEET	come into the presence of	OBIT	an obituary
MELT	change from a solid to a liquid state by heat	OCTET	a group of eight
		OFT	often
MERIT	to earn	OMIT	to leave out
MET	past tense of meet	ONSET	a beginning
MIDST	the middle	OOT	out
MIGHT	strength	OPT	to choose
MILT	impregnate with fish sperm	ORBIT	to revolve around
MINT	to produce by stamping metal as coins	ORT	a scrap of food
		OUGHT	to owe
MIST	to become blurry	OUST	to remove from a position or place
MITT	a type of baseball glove		
MIXT	past tense of mix	OUT	to be revealed
MOAT	a water filled trench	OVERT	open to view
MOIST	slightly wet	OWLET	a young owl
MOLT	cast off outer covering	PACT	an agreement
MOOT	bring up for discussion	PAINT	coloring substances
MORT	a note sounded on a hunting horn	PALET	palea – grass flower
		PANT	to breathe quickly
MOST	the greatest amount	PART	to divide into pieces
MOT	a witty saying	PAST	time gone by
MOTET	a choral composition	PAT	to touch lightly
MOTT	motte	PEART	lively
MOULT	to molt	PEAT	partially decayed vegetable matter
MOUNT	to get up on		
MULCT	to defraud	PELT	strike repeatedly with blows or missiles
MUST	to become musty		
MUT	mutt	PENT	confined
MUTT	a mongrel dog	PERT	impudent
NEAT	a state of cleanliness	PEST	annoying person
NEIST	next	PET	to caress with the hand
NEST	structure for bird eggs	PETIT	small minor
NET	type of openwork fabric	PEWIT	the lapwing
NETT	to net	PHAT	susceptible of easy and rapid typesetting
NEWT	a small salamander		
NEXT	coming immediately after	PHOT	a unit of illumination
NIGHT	the period from sunset to sunrise	PHT	expression of mild anger
		PICOT	edge with ornamental loop
NIT	egg of a parasitic insect	PILOT	to control the course of
NOT	in no way	PINT	a measure of capacity

PIPET	to pipette	RAMET	independent member of a clone
PIPIT	a songbird		
PIT	cavities or depressions	RANT	speak in a loud or vehement manner
PIVOT	to turn on a shaft or rod		
PLAIT	to braid	RAPT	deeply engrossed
PLANT	to place in the ground for growing	RAT	long tailed rodents
		REACT	to respond to a stimulus
PLAT	to plait	REBUT	to refute
PLEAT	fold in an even manner	REEST	to balk
PLOT	to plan secretly	REFIT	repair equipment for additional use
POET	one who writes poems		
POINT	indicate direction with the finger *RELIT*	REFT	past tense of reave
		REMIT	send money in payment
PORT	to shift to the left side	RENT	to obtain temporary
POSIT	to place	REST	to refresh oneself by ceasing work or activity
POST	to affix in a public place		
POT	round fairly deep container	RET	soak to loosen fiber from the woody tissue
POULT	a young domestic fowl		
POUT	protrude lips in ill humor	REVET	to face with masonry
PRAT	the buttocks	RIANT	cheerful
PREST	a loan	RIFT	clefts
PRINT	pressed type on surface	RIGHT	in accordance with what is good or just
PROST	prosit – a toast		
PSST	used to attract attention	RIOT	violent public disturbance
PUNT	propel through water with a pole	RIVET	fasten with metal bolt
		ROAST	to cook with dry heat
PUT	place in a particular position	ROBOT	humanlike machine
		ROOST	settle down or sleep
PUTT	a light stroke in golf	ROOT	underground portion of a plant
QAT	leaves of Catha edulis		
QANAT	type of water management system	ROSET	resin
		ROT	to decompose
QUANT	propel through water with a pole	ROUST	to arouse and drive out
		ROUT	defeat overwhelmingly
QUART	measure of capacity	RUNT	a small person or animal
QUEST	to make a search	RUST	reddish coating that forms on iron
QUIET	making little or no noise		
QUILT	stitch together with padding in between	RUT	grooves
		RYOT	a tenant farmer in India
QUINT	a group of five	SABOT	a wooden shoe
QUIRT	strike with a riding whip	SAINT	a person of exceptional holiness
QUIT	to stop doing something		
QUOIT	a throwing game	SALT	a crystalline seasoning
RAFT	a buoyant structure	SAT	past tense of sit

SAULT	a waterfall	SKINT	having no money
SCANT	meager	SKIRT	to go or pass around
SCART	to scratch	SKIT	a short dramatic scene
SCAT	to leave hastily	SLANT	deviate from the horizontal
SCATT	a tax		or vertical
SCENT	to fill with an odor	SLAT	narrow strips of wood or
SCOOT	to go quickly		metal
SCOT	a tax	SLEET	frozen rain
SCOUT	observe for the purpose of	SLEPT	past tense of sleep
	obtaining information	SLIPT	past tense of slip
SCUT	a short tail as of a rabbit	SLIT	a long narrow cut
SEAT	something to sit upon	SLOT	a long narrow opening
SECT	group of people united by	SLUT	a slovenly woman
	common beliefs	SMALT	a blue pigment
SENT	past tense of send	SMART	a sharp stinging pain
SEPT	a clan	SMELT	to melt or fuse as ores
SET	put particular position	SMOLT	a young salmon
SEXT	one of seven canonical	SMUT	to soil
	daily periods for prayer	SNIT	a state of agitation
SHAFT	to propel with a pole	SNOOT	to treat with disdain
SHAT	past tense of shit	SNORT	to exhale noisily through
SHEET	thin rectangular piece of		the nostrils
	material	SNOT	nasal mucus
SHIFT	move to another position	SNOUT	to provide with a nozzle
SHIRT	a garment for the upper	SOFT	yielding to pressure
	part of the body	SOOT	substance produced by
SHIST	schist		combustion
SHIT	to defecate - crude	SORT	to arrange according to
SHOAT	a young hog		kind, class or size
SHOOT	discharge a missile from a	SOT	an habitual drunkard
	weapon	SPAIT	spate
SHORT	having little length	SPAT	to strike lightly
SHOT	small lead or steel pellets	SPELT	a variety of wheat
SHOTT	chott	SPENT	past tense of spend
SHOUT	to utter loudly	SPILT	past tense of spill
SHUNT	to turn aside	SPIRT	to spurt
SHUT	to close	SPIT	rod on which meat is
SIFT	to sieve		turned
SIGHT	to observe or notice	SPLAT	piece of wood forming the
SILT	sedimentary material		middle of chair back
SIT	to rest on the buttocks	SPLIT	to separate lengthwise
SKAT	a card game	SPORT	to frolic
SKEET	the sport of shooting at	SPOT	small roundish
	clay pigeons		discolorations

124

SPOUT	eject in a rapid stream	TEMPT	entice to commit an
SPRAT	a small herring		unwise act
SPRIT	a ship's spar	TENET	principle belief or doctrine
SPURT	to gush forth		held to be true
SQUAT	to sit at one's heels	TENT	type of portable shelter
START	to set out	TEST	an examination
STET	cancel a previous made	TEXT	main body of a written or
	printing correction		printed work
STILT	long slender poles	THAT	the one indicated
STINT	to limit	THEFT	the act of stealing
STOAT	type of weasel	TIGHT	firmly
STOPT	past tense of stop	TILT	to cause to slant
STOUT	fat	TINCT	to tinge
STRUT	walk with a pompous air	TINT	to color slightly
STUNT	hinder normal growth	TIT	a small bird
STURT	contention	TOAST	brown by exposure to heat
SUET	hard fatty tissue around	TOFT	a hillock
	kidneys of cattle	TOIT	to saunter
SUINT	natural grease in the wool	TOOT	to sound a horn in short
	of sheep		blasts
SUIT	to be appropriate to	TORT	a civil wrong
SWART	swarthy	TOST	past tense of toss
SWAT	to hit sharply	TOT	to total
SWEAT	to perspire	TOUT	to solicit brazenly
SWEET	pleasing to the taste	TRACT	an expanse of land
SWEPT	past tense of sweep	TRAIT	distinguishing
SWIFT	moving with a great rate of		characteristic
	motion	TRAPT	past tense of trap
SWOT	to swat	TREAT	behave in a certain way
TACET	silent used as a musical	TRET	a support for a bridge
	direction	TROT	gait between walk and run
TACIT	unspoken	TROUT	a freshwater fish
TACT	skill in dealing with delicate	TRUST	to place confidence in
	situations	TRYST	to agree to meet
TAINT	to affect with something	TUFT	clusters of flexible
	bad		outgrowths
TAROT	playing cards used for	TUT	exclamation of impatience
	fortune telling	TWAT	the vulva usually vulgar
TART	a sharp sour taste	TWEET	to chirp
TAT	to make tatting	TWIST	to combine by winding
TAUNT	challenge sarcastically	TWIT	to ridicule
TAUT	fully stretched	TWIXT	between
TEAT	a mammary gland	UIT	out of
		UNFIT	to make unsuitable

UNGOT	ungotten	WEST	cardinal point on compass
UNHAT	to remove one's hat	WET	saturated with a liquid
UNIT	quantity used as a standard of measurement	WHAT	true nature of something
		WHET	to sharpen by friction
UNLET	not rented	WHIPT	past tense of whip
UNSET	to unsettle	WHIST	to hush
UNWIT	to make insane	WHIT	a particle
UPSET	to overturn	WHORT	an edible berry
UT	musical tone C in the French solmization system	WIGHT	a living being
		WILT	to become limp
VALET	a personal servant	WIST	to know
VAST	extent or size	WIT	intelligence
VAT	large container for holding liquids	WONT	to make accustomed to
		WORST	to defeat
VAULT	an arched ceiling	WORT	plant, herb, or vegetable
VAUNT	to brag	WOST	of wit
VELDT	a grassland of southern Africa	WOT	to know
		WRAPT	past tense of wrap
VENT	opening for the escape of gas or liquid	WREST	to take away by force
		WRIST	junction between hand and forearm
VERST	Russian measure of distance		
		WRIT	a written legal order
VERT	the heraldic color green	WURST	sausage
VEST	to place in the control of	XYST	a covered portico
VET	treat animals medically	YACHT	vessel for pleasure cruising or racing
VEXT	past tense of vex		
VISIT	to visit someone	YEAST	to foam
WAFT	float lightly over water	YET	up to now
WAIST	part body between the ribs and the hips	YETT	agate
		YURT	a portable tent
WAIT	to stay in expectation	ZEST	invigorating excitement
WANT	to have a desire for	ZIBET	an Asian civet
WART	protuberance on skin		
WAST	west		
WAT	wet or a hare		
WATT	a unit of power		
WECHT	weight		
WEEST	superlative of wee		
WEET	to know		
WEFT	a woven fabric		
WELT	lumps raised on the skin		
WENT	past tense of go		
WEPT	past tense of weep		
WERT	past tense of be		

U

ADIEU	farewell
AMU	a unit of mass
BABU	baboo
BATTU	a ballet movement
BAYOU	a marshy body of water
BEAU	a boyfriend
BIJOU	a jewel
CORNU	hornlike bone formation
COYPU	an aquatic rodent
EAU	water
ECRU	a yellowish brown color
ECU	an old French coin
EMEU	emu
EMU	a large flightless bird
FEU	grant land to under Scottish feudal law
FLU	a virus disease
FONOU	fondue
FOU	drunk
GENU	the knee
GNU	a large antelope
GURU	a Hindu spiritual teacher
HABU	a poisonous snake
HAIKU	a Japanese poem
HOKKU	haiku
IGLU	igloo
JEHU	a fast driver
JEU	a game
JUJU	having magical power
KAGU	a flightless bird
KUDU	a large antelope
KUDZU	an Asian vine
KURU	disease nervous system
LEU	monetary unit of Rumania
LIEU	place; stead
LITU	former monetary unit of Lithuania
LUAU	a Hawaiian feast
LULU	something remarkable
MENU	food available in a restaurant
MIAOU	to meow
MU	a Greek letter
NU	a Greek letter
PAREU	a Polynesian garment
PERDU	a soldier sent on a dangerous mission
PILAU	pilaf
PIU	used as a musical direction
POILU	a French soldier
PRAHU	prau
PRAU	Malaysian sailing vessel
QUIPU	an ancient calculating device
SADHU	a Hindu holy man
SAJOU	a capuchin
SNAFU	state of confusion
SOU	a former French coin
TABU	to taboo
TAU	a Greek letter
THOU	you
THRU	through
TOFU	Oriental soy milk cheese
TOLU	a fragrant resin
TUTU	a short ballet skirt
UNAU	a two toed sloth
VAU	vav
VERTU	virtu
VIRTU	love or taste for the fine arts
WAEFU	waeful
XU	monetary unit of Vietnam
YOU	2nd person pronoun
ZEBU	an Asian ox

V

DEV	veva
GANEV	unscrupulous opportunist
LEV	monetary unit of Bulgaria
REV	to increase the speed
SCHAV	a chilled soup
SHIV	a knife
SPIV	a petty criminal
TAV	a Hebrew letter
VAV	a Hebrew letter

LAV
LUV
Perv
NAV

AGLOW	glowing	ELBOW	to jostle
ALLOW	put no obstacle in the way	EMBOW	to arch
ALOW	in or to a lower position	ENDOW	provide with something
ANEW	once more	ENOW	enough
ARROW	symbol to indicate the proper direction	FEW	consisting of a small number
ASKEW	to one side	FLAW	an imperfection
AVOW	to declare openly	FLEW	a fishing net
AW	used to express disbelief	FLOW	to move steadily and smoothly along
BEDEW	to wet with dew		
BELOW	beneath	FROW	froe
BLAW	to blow	GLOW	to emit light and heat
BLEW	past tense of blow	GNAW	wear away by persistent biting
BLOW	drive or impel by a current of air		
		GREW	past tense of grow
BOW	to bend forward	GROW	to cultivate
BRAW	splendid	HAW	to turn left
BREW	to make beer or the like	HEW	to cut with an ax
BROW	the forehead	HOW	a method of doing something
BYLAW	a secondary law		
CAHOW	a sea bird	INDOW	to endow
CAW	the sound of a crow	JAW	to jabber
CHAW	to chew	JEW	a Hebrew
CHEW	to crush with the teeth	JOW	to toll
CHOW	to eat	KNEW	past tense of know
CLAW	sharp, curved toenails	KNOW	have true understanding
CLEW	to roll into a ball	KOTOW	to kowtow
COW	a farm animal	LAW	system of rules
CRAW	the stomach of certain animals	LOW	having relatively little upward extension
CREW	to serve abroad a ship	MACAW	a large parrot
CROW	to boast	MAW	to mow
DAW	to dawn	MEOW	sound of a cat
DEW	condensed moisture	MEW	to confine
DHOW	an Arabian sailing vessel	MIAOW	to meow
DOW	to prosper	MOW	cut standing herbage
DRAW	to move by pulling	NEW	not existing before
DREW	past tense of draw	NOHOW	in no manner

NOW	the present time	TAW	convert into white leather using minerals
OW	expression of sudden pain		
OXBOW	U shaped piece of wood	TEW	to work hard
PAPAW	a fleshy fruit	THAW	to melt
PAW	to strike or scrape with a beating motion	THEW	a well-developed muscle
		THRAW	to twist
PEW	a church bench	THREW	past tense of throw
PHEW	used to express relief	THROW	propel through the air with a movement of the arm
PILAW	pilaf		
PLOW	a farm implement	TOW	pull by means of a rope or chain
POW	an explosive sound		
PROW	forward part of a ship	TROW	to suppose
PSHAW	expression of disapproval	UNMEW	to set free
RAW	uncooked	UNSEW	to undo the sewing of
RENEW	to make new	VAW	vav
ROW	propel by means of oars	VIEW	to look at
SAW	type of cutting tool	WAW	vav
SCOW	flat bottomed boat	WHEW	a whistling sound
SCREW	type of metal fastener	WIDOW	to deprive of a husband
SEROW	a Asian antelope	WOW	to excite enthusiastic approval
SEW	to mend or fasten with a needle and thread		
		YAW	deviate from an intended course
SHAW	to show		
SHEW	to show	YEW	evergreen tree or shrub
SHOW	to cause to be seen	YOW	to yowl
SHREW	to curse		
SINEW	to strengthen		
SKEW	to turn aside		
SLAW	coleslaw		
SLEW	to slue		
SLOW	moving with little speed		
SMEW	a Eurasian duck		
SNAW	very stylish		
SNOW	precipitation in the form of ice crystals		
SOW	scatter seeds over land		
SPEW	to vomit		
SQUAW	American Indian woman		
STAW	past tense of steal		
STEW	to cook by boiling slowly		
STOW	to pack		
STRAW	stalks of threshed grain		
STREW	to scatter about		
STROW	to strew		

X - END

ADDAX	a large antelope		HELIX	something spiral in form
ADMIX	to mix		HEX	to cast an evil spell
AFFIX	to attach		HOAX	to deceive
ANNEX	to add or attach		HYRAX	small hare like mammal
APEX	the highest point		IBEX	a wild goat
AX	a type of cutting tool		ILEX	of ilium
BEAUX	of beau		IMMIX	to mix in
BEMIX	to mix thoroughly		INDEX	reference guide at the end of a book
BORAX	white crystalline compound		INFIX	to implant
BOX	a rectangle container		JINX	to bring bad luck
CALIX	a cup		KEX	a dry hollow stalk
CALX	a mineral residue		KYLIX	a drinking vessel
CALYX	protective covering of a flower		LATEX	a milky liquid of certain plants
CAREX	a marsh plant		LAX	not strict or stringent
CIMEX	a bedbug		LEX	law
COAX	to cajole		LOX	liquid oxygen
CODEX	an ancient manuscript		LUX	a unit of illumination
COX	to coxswain		LYNX	a short tailed wildcat
CRUX	a basic or decisive point		MINX	a flirtatious girt
CULEX	a mosquito		MIREX	an insecticide
CYLIX	kylix		MIX	put together in one mass
DESEX	to castrate or spray		MUREX	a marine mollusk
DEWAX	to remove wax from		MUX	session management protocol
DEX	central nervous system stimulant		NIX	to veto
EX	the letter X		OBEX	part of human brain
FAX	to reproduce by electronic means		ONYX	a variety of quartz
			ORYX	an African antelope
FIX	to repair		OX	a hoofed mammal
FLAX	an annual herb		PAX	ceremonial embrace to signify love and unit
FLEX	to bend			
FLUX	to melt		PHLOX	a flowering plant
FOX	to outwit		PIX	pyx
GALAX	an evergreen herb		POX	to infect with syphilis
GOX	gaseous oxygen		PREX	a president
HAPAX	word that occurs only once		PYREX	a type of dish

PLEX

131

PYX	a container for the Eucharistic bread
RADIX	the root of a plant
RAX	to stretch out
REDOX	type of chemical reaction
RELAX	make less tense or rigid
REMEX	flight feather of a bird's wing
REX	king
ROUX	mixture of butter and flour
SALIX	type of tree
SAX	a saxophone
SENEX	old, aged
SEX	to determine the sex
SILEX	silica
SIOUX	an Indian tribe
SIREX	a wood wasp
SIX	a number
SOX	of sock
SPHEX	type of wasp
STRIX	genus of owls
TAX	fee imposed for public purposes
TELEX	to send a message by a telegraphic system
TEXT	written language
TUX	a tuxedo
ULEX	type of thorny plant
UNBOX	to remove from a box
UNFIX	to unfasten
UNSEX	to deprive sexual power
VARIX	a varicose vein
VEX	to annoy
VIBEX	subcutaneous effusion of blood
VIVAX	species of malaria
WAX	heat sensitive substance
XEROX	to make copy
YEX	hiccup
YOX	yex
YUNX	genus of birds
ZAX	a tool for cutting roof slates

X - ALL

ADDAX	a large antelope		BUXOM	healthily plump
ADMIX	to mix		CALIX	a cup
AFFIX	to attach		CALX	a mineral residue
ANNEX	to add or attach		CALYX	protective covering of a flower
APEX	the highest point			
ATAXY	ataxia		CAREX	a marsh plant
AUXIN	a substance to regulate plant growth		CIMEX	a bedbug
			COAX	to cajole
AX	a type of cutting tool		CODEX	an ancient manuscript
AXAL	to axial		COX	to coxswain
AXE	to ax		COXA	the hip or hip joint
AXEL	jump in figure skating		COXAL	type of gland
AXIAL	pertaining to or forming an axis		CRUX	a basic or decisive point
			CULEX	a mosquito
AXIL	angle between the upper side of a leaf and its supporting stem		CYLIX	kylix
			DESEX	to castrate or spray
			DEWAX	to remove wax from
AXILE	axial		DEX	central nervous system stimulant
AXIOM	a self-evident truth			
AXION	hypothetical elementary particle		DIXIT	a statement
			DOXIE	doxy
AXIS	a straight line about which a body rotates		DOXY	a doctrine
			EPOXY	a type of resin
AXITE	a fiber of an axon		EX	the letter X
AXLE	shaft upon which a wheel revolves		EXACT	precise
			EXALT	to raise
AXMAN	one who wields an ax		EXAM	an examination
AXON	the central process of a neuron		EXCEL	to surpass others
			EXEC	an executive officer
AXONE	axon		EXERT	to put into action
BEAUX	of beau		EXILE	to banish from one's own country
BEMIX	to mix thoroughly			
BORAX	a white crystalline compound		EXINE	outer layer of certain spores
BOX	a rectangle container		EXIST	to be
BOXER	one that packs boxes		EXIT	to go out
BOXY	resembling a box		EXPEL	to force out
BRAXY	a fever of sheep		EXON	nucleic acid sequence

EXPEL	to drive or force out	LOX	liquid oxygen
EXPO	a public exhibition	LUX	a unit of illumination
EXTOL	to praise highly	LUXE	luxury
EXTRA	something additional	LYNX	a short tailed wildcat
EXULT	to rejoice greatly	MAXI	a long skirt or coat
EXURB	residential area beyond the suburbs of a city	MAXIM	brief statement of a general truth
FAX	reproduce by electronic means	MINX	a flirtatious girt
		MIREX	an insecticide
FIX	to repair	MIX	put together into one mass
FIXER	one that fixes	MIXER	one that mixes
FIXT	past tense of fix	MIXT	past tense of mix
FLAX	an annual herb	MIXUP	a state of confusion
FLAXY	flaxen	MOXA	a Chinese plant
FLEX	to bend	MOXIE	spirit of courage
FLUX	to melt	MUREX	a marine mollusk
FOX	to outwit	NEXT	coming immediately after; adjoining
FOXY	craftily	
GALAX	an evergreen herb	NEXUS	a connection or link
GOX	gaseous oxygen	NIX	to veto
HAPAX	word that occurs only once	NIXIE	a female water sprite
HEUX	something spiral in form	NIXY	undeliverable piece of mail
HEX	to cast an evil spell upon	ONYX	a variety of quartz
HEXAD	a group of six	ORYX	an African antelope
HEXER	one that hexes	OX	a hoofed mammal
HEXYL	a hydrocarbon radical	OXBOW	U shaped piece of wood
HOAX	to deceive	OXEN	plural of ox
HYRAX	small hare like mammal	OXEYE	a flowering plant
IBEX	a wild goat	OXID	oxide
ILEX	of ilium	OXIDE	compound of oxygen with another element
IMMIX	to mix in	
INDEX	reference guide at the end of a book	OXIM	oxime
		OXIME	a chemical compound
INFIX	to implant	OXLIP	a flowering plant
IXIA	a flowering plant	OXTER	the armpit
IXTLE	istle	OXY	containing oxygen
JINX	to bring bad luck	PAX	ceremonial embrace given to signify love and unity
KEX	a dry hollow stalk	
KYLIX	a drinking vessel	PHLOX	a flowering plant
LATEX	milky liquid of certain plants	PIX	pyx
		PIXIE	pixy
LAX	not strict or stringent	PIXY	a playfully mischievous fairy or elf
LAXLY	in a lax manner	
LEX	law	POX	to infect with syphilis

PREX	prexy	TOXIN	a poisonous substance
PREXY	a president	TUX	a tuxedo
PROXY	a person authorized to act for another	TWIXT	between
		UNBOX	to remove from a box
PYX	container the where Eucharistic bread is kept	UNFIX	to unfasten
		UNSEX	to deprive sexual power
PYXIE	an evergreen shrub	VARIX	a varicose vein
PYXIS	a pyxidium	VEX	to annoy
RADIX	the root of a plant	VEXER	one that vexes
RAX	to stretch out	VEXIL	vexillum
REDOX	a type of chemical reaction	VEXT	past tense of vex
RELAX	to make less tense	VIXEN	a shrewish woman
REMEX	a flight feather of a bird's wing	WAX	a natural, heat-sensitive substance
REX	king	WAXEN	covered with wax
ROUX	mixture of butter and flour	WAXER	one that waxes
SAX	a saxophone	WAXY	resembling wax
SEX	to determine the sex	XEBEC	a Mediterranean sailing vessel
SEXT	one of seven canonical daily periods for prayer	XENIA	foreign or strange
		XENIC	pertaining to a type of culture medium
SEXTO	sixmo		
SEXY	arousing sexual desire	XENON	a gaseous element
SILEX	silica	XERIC	requiring only a small amount of moisture
SIX	a number		
SIXMO	a paper size	XEROX	to make copy
SIXTE	a fencing parry	XERUS	African ground squirrel
SIXTH	one of six equal parts	XI	a Greek letter
SIXTY	a number	XU	monetary unit of Vietnam
SOX	of sock	XYLAN	a substance found in cell walls of plants
TAX	fee imposed for public purposes		
		XYLOL	xylene
TAXA	of taxon	XYLYL	a univalent radical
TAXER	one that taxes	XYST	xystus
TAXI	to travel in a taxicab	ZAX	tool for cutting roof slates
TAXON	a unit of scientific classification		
TAXUS	evergreen tree or shrub		
TELEX	send a message by telegraphic system		
TEXAS	the uppermost structure on a steamboat		
TEXT	main body of a written or printed work		
TOXIC	pertaining to a toxin		

Y

ABBEY	a monastery or convent	ATONY	muscular weakness
ABLY	in an able manner	ATOPY	a type of allergy
ABY	pay the penalty for	AWAY	from a certain place
ACHY	aching	AWRY	with a turn or twist to one side
ACIDY	sour		
AERY	airy	AY	aye
AGLY	agley	BABY	to coddle
AGONY	extreme pain	BADDY	baddie
AHOY	to hail a ship or person	BADLY	in a bad manner
AIRY	having the nature of air	BAFFY	a wooden golf club
ALARY	alar	BAGGY	loose-fitting
ALLEY	a narrow passageway	BALKY	stubborn
ALLOY	a homogenous mixture of metals	BALLY	damned
		BALMY	mild
ALLY	to unite in a formal relationship	BANDY	to throw to and fro
		BARKY	tough outer covering of a root or stem
AMBRY	recess in a church wall for sacred vessels		
		BARMY	frothy
AMITY	friendship	BARNY	resembling a barn in size or shape, or smell
ANGRY	feeling strong displeasure or hostility		
		BASSY	low in pitch
ANNOY	to be troublesome to	BATTY	crazy
ANOMY	anomie	BAWDY	obscene
ANY	one, no matter which	BAWTY	bawtie
APERY	the act of aping	BAY	to howl
APPLY	to bring into contact with something	BEADY	resembling beads
		BEAKY	resembling a beak
APTLY	in an apt manner	BEAMY	beaming
ARMY	body of men trained and armed for war	BEEFY	brawny
		BEIGY	of the color beige
ARRAY	place in proper or desired order	BELAY	to fasten a rope
		BENDY	okra
ARTY	showily or pretentiously artist	BERRY	to produce berries
		BEVY	a group
ASHY	covered with ashes	BEY	a Turkish ruler
ASSAY	to attempt	BIALY	an onion roll
ATAXY	ataxia	BIDDY	a hen
ATOMY	a tiny particle	BIFFY	a toilet

BIGLY	in a big manner	BURY	to put in the ground and cover with earth
BILGY	smelling like seepage		
BILLY	a short club	BUSBY	a tall fur hat
BITSY	tiny	BUSHY	covered with bushes
BITTY	fragmented	BUSTY	full-bosomed
BLIMY	expression when something goes wrong	BUSY	occupied
		BUTTY	a fellow workman
BLOWY	windy	BUY	to purchase
BLUEY	a bag of clothing carried in travel	BY	a pass in certain card games
BOBBY	a policeman	BYWAY	a side road
BODY	to give form to	CABBY	a driver of a cab
BOGEY	to shoot in one stroke over par in golf	CADDY	to caddie
		CADGY	cheerful
BOGGY	marshy	CAGEY	shrewd and careful
BOGY	a goblin	CAGY	cagey
BONEY	bony	CAMPY	comically exaggerated
BONNY	pretty	CANDY	confection made with sugar
BONY	full of bones		
BOOMY	prospering	CANTY	cheerful
BOOTY	a rich gain or prize	CARNY	a carnival
BOOZY	drunken	CARRY	to convey from one place to another
BOSKY	wooded; bushy		
BOSSY	domineering	CASKY	resembling a cask
BOUSY	boozy	CATTY	catlike; spiteful
BOXY	resembling a box	CAVY	a short-tailed rodent
BOY	a male child	CAY	a small, low island
BRAKY	abounding in shrubs or ferns	CHARY	cautious
		CHEVY	to chase about
BRAXY	a fever of sheep	CHEWY	not easily chewed
BRAY	to utter a harsh cry	CHIVY	to chevy
BRINY	the sea	CHOKY	tending to cause choking
BROSY	smeared with brose	CITY	a large town
BUBBY	often considered vulgar	CIVVY	a civilian
BUDDY	a good friend	CLARY	an aromatic herb
BUFFY	yellowish-brown color	CLAY	fine-grained, earthly material
BUGGY	a light carriage		
BULGY	bulging	CLOY	to gratify beyond desire
BULKY	massive	COBBY	stocky
BULLY	to treat abusively	COCKY	arrogantly self-confident
BUMPY	of uneven surface	COLLY	blacken with coal dust
BUOY	a warning float	COLY	an African bird
BURLY	heavy and muscular	COMFY	comfortable
BURRY	prickly	COMMY	commie

CONEY	cony	DARKY	black person - derogatory term
CONKY	full of a tree fungus		
CONY	a rabbit	DASHY	stylish
COOEY	to cooee	DAUBY	smeary
COOKY	cookie	DAVY	a safety lamp
COOLY	coolie	DAY	the time between sunrise and sunset
COPY	to imitate		
CORBY	corbie	DEARY	darting
CORKY	corklike	DECAY	to decompose
CORNY	trite	DECOY	to lure into a trap
COSEY	a cozy	DECRY	to denounce
COSY	cozy	DEEDY	industrious
COVEY	a flock of birds	DEFY	resist openly and boldly
COWRY	a glossy seashell	DEIFY	to make a god of
COWY	suggestive of a cow	DEITY	a god or goddess
COY	shy	DELAY	to put off to a later time
COYLY	in a coy manner	DELLY	deli
COZEY	cozy	DEMY	a size of paper
COZY	snug and comfortable	DENY	declare to be untrue
CRAZY	insane	DERAY	disorderly revelry
CREPY	crepey	DERBY	a type of hat
CRONY	a close friend	DERRY	a meaningless word used as part of a chorus
CRY	to weep		
CUBBY	a small enclosed space	DEWY	moist with dew
CUDDY	a donkey	DEY	a former North African ruler
CULLY	lies to trick		
CUPPY	cuplike	DIARY	a personal journal
CURDY	curdied	DICEY	dangerous
CURLY	tending to curl	DICKY	dickey
CURRY	to prepare leather for use or sale	DIDY	a diaper
		DILLY	something remarkable
CURVY	curved	DINGY	dinghy
CUSHY	easy	DINKY	dinkey
CUTEY	self-consciously cute	DIPPY	foolish
CUTTY	a thickset girl	DIRTY	unclean
DADDY	father	DISHY	attractive
DAFFY	silly	DITTY	a short simple song
DAILY	a newspaper published every weekday	DIVVY	to divide
		DIZZY	a sensation of whirling
DAIRY	an establishment dealing in milk products	DOBY	dobie
		DODGY	evasive
DAISY	a flowering plant	DOGEY	dogie
DALLY	to waste time	DOGGY	a small dog
DANDY	fine	DOGY	dogie

DOILY	a small napkin	ELEGY	a mournful poem for one who is dead
DOLLY	a wheeled platform		
DONSY	donsie	ELMY	abounding in elms
DOOLY	doolee	EMBAY	to enclose in a bay
DOOZY	doozer	EMERY	a granular corundum
DOPEY	lethargic stupid	EMPTY	containing nothing
DOPY	dopey	ENEMY	one that is antagonistic toward another
DORMY	dormie		
DORTY	sullen	ENJOY	to receive pleasure from
DORY	a flat bottomed boat	ENSKY	to raise to the skies
DOTTY	crazy	ENTRY	a place of entrance
DOTY	stained by decay	ENVOY	a representative
DOWDY	lacking in stylishness	ENVY	to be envious of
DOWNY	soft	EPOXY	a type of resin
DOWRY	money or property a wife brings at marriage	ESPY	to catch sight of
		ESSAY	tatty
DOXY	a doctrine	EVERY	each without exception
DOYLY	doily	EYRY	aerie
DOZY	drowsy	FADDY	faddish
DRAY	a low strong cart	FAERY	faerie
DRILY	dryly	FAIRY	an imaginary supernatural being
DRY	having no moisture		
DRYLY	in a dry manner	FANCY	to take a liking to
DUCHY	the domain of a duke	FANNY	the buttocks
DUCKY	excellent	FARCY	a disease of horses
DUDDY	duddie	FATLY	in the manner of one that is fat
DULY	rightfully		
DUMMY	a representation of	FATTY	greasy oily
DUMPY	short and thick	FAWNY	yellowish-brown color
DUNGY	filthy	FAY	to join closely
DUSKY	somewhat dark	FELLY	a felloe
DUSTY	full of dust	FENNY	marshy
DUTY	a moral or legal obligation	FERLY	something strange
EARLY	the beginning of a period of time of events	FERNY	abounding in ferns
		FERRY	a type of boat
EASY	not difficult	FEY	crazy
EBONY	a hard heavy wood	FIERY	intensely hot
EDDY	move against the main current	FIFTY	a number
		FILLY	a young female horse
EDGY	tense nervous or irritable	FILMY	covered with film
EDIFY	to enlighten	FINNY	having by fins
EELY	resembling an eel	FIRRY	abounding in firs
EERY	eerie	FISHY	of or resembling fish
		FITLY	in a fit manner

139

FIZZY	a hissing or sputtering sound	GABBY	talkative
		GABY	a dolt
FLAKY	resembling flakes	GAILY	in a gay manner
FLAMY	flaming	GALLY	to frighten
FLAWY	full of flaws	GAMEY	gamy
FLAXY	flaxen	GAMY	plucky
FLAY	to strip off the side of	GAPPY	having openings
FLEY	to frighten	GAPY	infested with gapeworms
FLUKY	happening by chance	GASSY	containing gas
FLUTY	resembling a flute in sound	GAUDY	tastelessly showy
FLY	to move through the air	GAUZY	resembling gauze
FLYBY	an aircraft close to a specified place	GAWKY	awkward
		GAWSY	gawsie
FOAMY	covered with foam	GAY	merry
FOGEY	fogy	GAYLY	in a gay manner
FOGGY	filled with fog	GEMMY	resembling a gem
FOGY	an old-fashioned person	GERMY	full of germs
FOLLY	a foolish idea or action	GEY	very
FOOTY	paltry	GIDDY	dizzy
FORAY	to raid	GILLY	a type of wagon
FORBY	close by	GIMPY	limping
FORKY	resembling a fork	GINNY	affected with gin
FORTY	a number	GIPSY	to gypsy
FOXY	crafty	GIRLY	featuring scantily clothed women
FOY	a farewell feast or gift		
FOZY	too ripe	GLADY	having glades
FRAY	to wear off by rubbing	GLARY	glaring
FRY	cook over direct heat in hot fat or oil	GLAZY	covered with a smooth, glossy coating
FUBSY	chubby and somewhat squat	GLEY	a soil layer
		GLORY	to rejoice proudly
FUGGY	stuffy and odorous	GLUEY	resembling glue
FULLY	in a full manner	GOBY	a small fish
FUMY	producing or full of fumes	GODLY	pious
FUNKY	having an offensive odor	GOLLY	used as a mild oath
FUNNY	causing laughter or amusement	GOODY	a desirable food
		GOOEY	sticky or viscid
FURRY	covered with fur	GOOFY	silly
FURY	violent anger	GOONY	gooney
FURZY	abounding in gorse	GOOSY	resembling a goose
FUSSY	overly concerned with small details	GORSY	abounding in gorse
		GORY	bloody
FUSTY	musty	GOUTY	affected with gout
FUZZY	blurry	GOY	a non-Jewish person

GRAPY	resembling grapes	HEY	used to attract attention
GRAVY	a sauce of the fat and juices from cooked meat	HILLY	abounding in hills
		HINNY	to whinny
GRAY	color between white and black	HIPPY	having big hips
		HOAGY	hoagie
GREY	gray	HOARY	white with age
GRIMY	dirty	HOBBY	a recreational pastime
GRIPY	causing sharp pains in the bowels	HOKEY	false; contrived
		HOLEY	full of holes
GULFY	full of whirlpools	HOLLY	a tree
GULLY	to form ravines by the action of water	HOLY	having a divine nature
		HOMEY	homelike
GULPY	marked by gulping	HOMY	homey
GUMMY	resembling gum	HONEY	a sweet viscid fluid
GUNNY	a coarse fabric	HONKY	honkie
GUPPY	a small tropical fish	HOOEY	something false or nonsensical
GURRY	fish offal		
GUSHY	overly sentimental	HOOKY	truancy or full of hooks
GUSTY	blowing in gusts	HOOLY	in a gentle manner
GUTSY	brave	HORNY	hornlike in hardness
GUTTY	marked by courage	HORSY	resembling a horse
GUY	to ridicule	HOTLY	in a hot manner
GYPSY	a wanderer	HOWDY	howdie
HAIRY	covered with hair	HOY	a heavy barge or scow
HAMMY	overly theatrical	HUBBY	a husband
HANDY	convenient for handling	HUFFY	easily offended
HANKY	a handkerchief	HULKY	massive
HAPLY	by chance	HUMPY	full of humps
HAPPY	marked by joy	HUNKY	an unskilled laborer
HARDY	very sturdy	HURLY	commotion
HARPY	a shrewish person	HURRY	to move swiftly
HARRY	to pillage	HUSKY	an Eskimo dog
HASTY	speedy	HUSSY	a lewd woman
HAY	grass cut and dried for fodder	ICILY	in an icy manner
		ICKY	repulsive
HAZY	unclear	ICY	covered with ice
HEADY	intoxicating	IDLY	in an idle manner
HEAVY	having much weight	IFFY	full of uncertainty
HEDGY	abounding in hedges	ILLY	badly
HEFTY	heavy	IMMY	a type of playing marble
HEMPY	mischievous	IMPLY	to indicate or suggest directly
HENRY	a unit of inductance		
HERBY	abounding in herbs	INBY	inward
HERRY	to harry	INKY	resembling ink

INLAY	to set into a surface	KITTY	a kitten or cat
INLY	inwardly	KOOKY	eccentric
IRONY	express the opposite of what is literally said	LACEY	lacy
		LACY	resembling lacework
ITCHY	an itching sensation	LADY	woman of refinement and gentle manners
IVORY	substance in elephant tusks		
		LAITY	non-clerical member of a religious faith
IVY	a climbing vine		
JACKY	a sailor	LAKY	of the color bleed
JAGGY	jagged	LANKY	ungracefully tall & thin
JANTY	jaunty	LARDY	resembling lard
JAY	a corvine bird	LARKY	playful
JAZZY	lively	LATHY	long & slender
JELLY	soft semisolid substance	LAXLY	in a lax manner
JEMMY	to jimmy	LAY	to deposit as a wager
JENNY	a female donkey	LAZY	disinclined to work or exertion
JERKY	characterized by jerking movements		
		LEADY	resembling lead
JERRY	a German soldier	LEAFY	covered with leaves
JETTY	to jut	LEAKY	tending to leak
JIFFY	a short time	LEARY	leery
JIMMY	open with a crowbar	LEAVY	leafy
JIMPY	jimp	LEDGY	abounding in ledges
JOEY	a young kangaroo	LEERY	suspicious
JOLLY	cheerful	LEFTY	a left-handed person
JOLTY	marked by a jolting motion	LEGGY	having long legs
JOTTY	written down quickly	LEVY	to impose or collect by legal authority
JOWLY	having prominent jowls		
JOY	to rejoice	LEY	lea
JUICY	full of juice	LILY	a flowering plant
JUMPY	nervous	LIMBY	having many large branches
JUNKY	worthless		
JURY	a group sworn to render a verdict	LIMEY	a British sailor
		LIMY	containing lime
JUTTY	to jut	LINDY	a lively dance
KAURY	kauri	LINEY	liny
KAY	the letter K	LINGY	covered with heaths
KELPY	kelpie	LINKY	full of interlocking rings
KERRY	an Irish breed of cattle	LINTY	covered with lint
KEY	a device used to turn the bolt in a lock	LINY	resembling a line
		LIPPY	impudent
KIDDY	kiddie	LOAMY	resembling loam
KILTY	kiltie	LOBBY	to attempt to influence legislators
KINKY	tightly curled		

LOFTY	extending high in the air	MIDDY	a loosely fitting blouse
LOGGY	logy	MIFFY	easily annoyed
LOGY	sluggish	MILKY	resembling of milk
LOLLY	a lollipop	MILTY	full of milt
LOOBY	a large awkward person	MINCY	affectedly dainty
LOOEY	looie	MINGY	mean and stingy
LOONY	crazy	MINNY	minnow
LOOPY	full of loops	MINTY	having the flavor mint
LOPPY	hanging limply	MIRKY	murky
LORRY	a type of wagon or truck	MIRY	swampy
LORY	a small parrot	MISSY	a young gin
LOSSY	causing dissipation of electrical energy	MISTY	blurry
		MITY	infested with mites
LOURY	lowery	MOLDY	musty
LOUSY	mean or contemptible	MOLLY	mollie
LOWLY	low in position or rank	MOLY	a wild garlic
LUCKY	having good fortune	MOMMY	mother
LUMPY	full of lumps	MONEY	a medium of exchange
LUNY	loony	MONY	many
LUSTY	full of vigor	MOODY	given to changing moods
MADLY	in a mad manner	MOONY	resembling the moon
MALMY	crumbly, chalky rock	MOORY	marshy
MALTY	resembling malt	MORAY	a tropical eel
MAMEY	a tropical tree	MOSEY	to saunter
MANGY	affected with mange	MOSSY	covered with moss
MANLY	having qualities of a man	MOTEY	full of motes
MANY	a large number	MOTHY	full of moths
MARLY	abounding with marl	MOUSY	resembling a mouse
MARRY	to enter into marriage	MUCKY	filthy
MASHY	mashie	MUDDY	covered with mud
MASSY	massive	MUHLY	a perennial grass
MATEY	a friend	MULEY	a hornless cow
MAY	used as an auxiliary to express permission	MUMMY	to mummify
		MURKY	dark
MAZY	full of confusing turns	MURRY	a moray
MEALY	soft dry and friable	MUSHY	pulpy
MEANY	meanie	MUSKY	resembling musk
MEATY	full of meat	MUSSY	messy
MEINY	a retinue	MUSTY	having a stale odor
MERCY	compassion shown to an offender or enemy	MUZZY	confused
		MY	form of the pronoun I
MERRY	cheerful	MYOPY	myopia
MESHY	netty	NANNY	a children's nurse
MESSY	dirty or untidy	NAPPY	kinky

NARY	not one	OVARY	female reproductive gland
NASTY	offensive to the senses	OXY	containing oxygen
NATTY	neatly	OY	used to express dismay or
NAVVY	a manual laborer		pain
NAVY	a nation's warships	PADDY	a rice field
NAY	a negative vote	PALLY	marked by close friendship
NEEDY	in a state of poverty	PALMY	marked by prosperity
NERVY	impudent	PALSY	to paralyze
NETTY	resembling a net	PALY	somewhat pale
NEWLY	recently	PANDY	to punish by striking the
NEWSY	full of news		hand
NIFTY	stylish; pleasing	PANSY	a flowering plant
NINNY	a fool	PANTY	pantie
NIPPY	sharp or biting	PAPPY	resembling pap or a father
NITTY	full of nits	PARDY	pardi
NIXY	an undeliverable piece of	PARRY	to ward of a blow
	mail	PASTY	pale and unhealthy in
NOBBY	elegant		appearance
NOBLY	in a noble manner	PATLY	suitably
NODDY	a fool	PATSY	person easily fooled
NOISY	making loud sounds	PATTY	a small flat cake or
NOOKY	sexual intercourse-		chopped food
	considered vulgar	PATY	formee
NOSEY	nosy	PAWKY	sly
NOSY	unduly curious	PAY	give money in exchange for
NOWAY	in no way		goods or services
NUBBY	having nubs	PEAKY	sickly
NUTTY	abounding in nuts	PEATY	resembling or containing
OBEY	to follow commands		peat
OCHRY	ochery	PEAVY	peavey
ODDLY	in an odd manner	PECKY	marked by decay caused by
OFAY	white person - usually		fungi
	taken to be offensive	PEERY	a child's toy
OILY	covered or soaked with oil	PENNY	a coin of the United
OKAY	to approve		Kingdom
OLOGY	a branch of knowledge	PEONY	a flowering plant
ONERY	ornery	PEPPY	full of energy
ONLY	with nothing or no one else	PERDY	pardi
OOZY	containing or resembling	PERKY	jaunty
	soft mud or slime	PERRY	a beverage of pear juice
ORGY	party marked by		often fermented
	unrestrained sexual	PESKY	annoying
	indulgence	PETTY	insignificant
OUTBY	outdoors	PHONY	not genuine or real

PICKY	fussy	PREY	to seize and devour
PIETY	state of being pious		animals for food
PIGGY	a small pig	PRICY	pricey
PIGMY	pygmy	PRIVY	private or an outhouse
PILY	divided Into wedge shaped	PROSY	prosaic
	heraldic designs	PROXY	a person authorized to act
PINEY	piny		for another
PINKY	pinkie	PRY	inquire impertinently into
PINY	suggestive of or covered		private matters
	with pine trees	PUDGY	short and fat
PIPY	shrill	PUFFY	swollen
PITHY	concise	PUGGY	puggish
PITY	sorrow aroused by	PULPY	resembling pulp
	another's misfortune	PUNKY	resembling punk
PIXY	playfully mischievous fairy	PUNNY	being or involving a pun
	or elf	PUNTY	iron rod used in fencing
PLATY	a small tropical fish	PUNY	inferior size, strength or
PLAY	engage in amusement or		significance
	sport	PUPPY	a young dog
PLOY	to move from a line into	PURSY	short of breath
	column	PUSHY	offensively aggressive
PLUMY	covered with feathers	PUSSY	a cat
PLY	supply with or offer	PUTTY	a type of cement
	repeatedly	PYGMY	a small person
POCKY	covered with pocks	QUAKY	lending to quake
PODGY	pudgy	QUAY	a wharf
POESY	poetry	QUERY	to question
POGEY	any form of government	QUEY	a young cow
	relief	RACY	bordering impropriety or
POGY	a marine fish		indecency
POKEY	poky	RAGGY	ragi
POKY	a jail	RAINY	marked by rain
POLY	type of white blood cell	RALLY	to come together for
PONY	study lessons with a literal		common purpose
	translation	RAMMY	rammish
POPPY	a flowering plant	RANDY	a rude person
PORGY	a marine food fish	RANGY	tall & slender
PORKY	resembling pork	RASPY	rough
POSY	a flower or bouquet	RATTY	infested with rats
POTSY	a children's game	RAWLY	in a raw manner
POTTY	of little importance	RAY	narrow beams of light
POUTY	tending to pout	READY	prepared
PRAY	to address prayers to	REDLY	with red color
PREXY	a president	REEDY	abounding in reeds

REEKY	reeking	SAURY	a marine fish
REIFY	to regard as real or concrete	SAVOY	a variety of cabbage
		SAVVY	to understand
RELAY	to send along	SAY	to utter
RELY	to place trust or confidence	SCALY	peeling off in flakes
REPAY	to pay back	SCARY	frightening
REPLY	to answer	SEAMY	unpleasant
RIBBY	curved bony rods in the body	SEDGY	abounding in sedge
		SEEDY	inferior in condition or quality
RIDGY	having ridges	
RILEY	angry	SEELY	frail
RIMY	frosty	SEEPY	soaked or oozing with water
RISKY	dangerous	
RITZY	elegant	SEPOY	native of India serving in the British army
ROCKY	unsteady	
ROILY	muddy	SERRY	to crowd together
ROOKY	abounding in rooks	SEXY	arousing sexual desire
ROOMY	spacious	SHADY	shaded
ROOTY	full of roots	SHAKY	shaking
ROPY	resembling a rope	SHALY	resembling shale
ROSY	rose colored	SHAY	a chaise
ROUPY	hoarse	SHILY	in a shy manner
ROWDY	disorderly in behavior	SHINY	filled with light
RUBY	red precious stone	SHOWY	making a great or brilliant display
RUDDY	having a healthy reddish color	SHY	timid
		SHYLY	in a shy manner
RUGBY	a form of football	SILKY	resembling silk
RUMMY	a card game	SILLY	a lack of good sense
RUMMY	odd	SILTY	full of silt
RUNNY	tending to drip	SISSY	effeminate man or boy
RUNTY	small	SIXTY	a number
RUSHY	abounding in rushes	SIZY	viscid
RUSTY	covered with rust	SKIEY	skyey
RUTTY	marked by ruts	SKY	the upper atmosphere
SADLY	in a sad manner	SKYEY	resembling the sky
SAGY	flavored with sage	SLATY	resembling slate
SALLY	to rush out suddenly	SLAY	to kill violently
SALTY	tasting of or containing salt	SULY	in a sly manner
SANDY	containing or covered with sand	SUMY	resembling slime
		SLY	crafty
SAPPY	silly	SMOKY	filled with smoke
SASSY	sasswood	SNAKY	resembling a snake
SAUCY	impudent	SNOWY	abounding in snow

RESAY

146

SOAPY	containing or resembling soap	SURFY	abounding in breaking waves
SODDY	a house built of sod	SURGY	surging
SOFTY	a sentimental person	SURLY	sullenly rude
SOGGY	heavy with moisture	SWAMY	swami
SONLY	pertaining to a son	SWAY	move back and forth
SONNY	a small boy	TABBY	to give a wavy appearance to
SONSY	comely		
SOOEY	used in calling pigs	TACKY	adhesive
SOOTY	covered with soot	TAFFY	a chewy candy
SOPHY	a ruler of Persia	TALKY	talks a great deal
SOPPY	very wet	TALLY	to count
SORRY	feeling grief or penitence	TAMMY	a fabric of mixed fibers
SOUPY	foggy	TANGY	pungent
SOY	the soybean	TANSY	a perennial herb
SPAY	to remove the ovaries	TARDY	late
SPICY	containing spices	TARRY	delay or be slow in acting or doing
SPIKY	resembling a spike		
SPINY	bearing or covered with thorns	TASTY	pleasant to the taste
		TATTY	shabby
SPIRY	tall slender and tapering	TAWNY	light brown
SPLAY	to spread out	TEARY	tearful
SPRAY	disperse in fine particles	TECHY	tetchy
SPRY	nimble	TEDDY	women's undergarment
SPUMY	foamy	TEENY	tiny
SPY	to watch secretly	TELLY	a television set
STAGY	having a theatrical quality	TENTY	watchful
STAY	to continue in a place	TERRY	an absorbent fabric
STEY	steep	TESTY	irritable
STIMY	to stymie	THEY	3rd person pronoun
STOGY	a long slender cigar	THY	thou
STONY	abounding in stones	THYMY	abounding in thyme
STORY	an account of an event or series of events	TIDY	neat & orderly
		TINNY	of or resembling tin
STRAY	wander from the proper area of course	TINY	very small
		TIPPY	unsteady
STROY	to destroy	TIPSY	slightly drunk
STUDY	to acquire knowledge	TITTY	a teat
STY	to keep in a pigpen	TIVY	with great speed
STYMY	to stymie	TIZZY	a state of nervous confusion
SUDSY	foamy		
SULKY	sullenly aloof or withdrawn	TOADY	to engage in servile flattering
SULLY	to soil		
		TOBY	a type of drinking mug

TODAY	the present day	VEALY	immature
TODDY	an alcoholic beverage	VEERY	a songbird
TODY	a West Indian bird	VEINY	full of veins
TOFFY	toffee	VERY	absolute
TOKAY	a Malaysian gecko	VICHY	type of mineral water
TOMMY	a loaf of bread	VIEWY	showy
TONY	stylish	VINY	covered with wine
TORY	a political conservative	WACKY	very irrational
TOWNY	townie	WADDY	strike with a thick club
TOWY	resembling coarse hemp or flax fiber	WADY	wadi
		WALLY	waly
TOY	a child's plaything	WALY	something visually pleasing
TRAY	a flat shallow receptacle	WANEY	waning or diminished in some parts
TREY	a three in cards, dice or dominoes		
		WANLY	in a wan manner
TROY	a system of weights	WANY	waning in some parts
TRULY	in conformity with fact or reality	WARTY	covered With warts
		WARY	watchful
TRY	to attempt	WASHY	overly diluted
TUBBY	short & fat	WASPY	resembling a wasp
TUFTY	abounding in tufts	WAVEY	the snow goose
TUMMY	the stomach	WAVY	full of waves
TUNNY	a tuna	WAXY	resembling wax
TURFY	covered with turf	WAY	a method of doing something
TUTTY	an impure zinc oxide		
TWINY	a strong string	WEARY	tired
TYPEY	typy	WEBBY	web like
TYPY	strict conformance to characteristics of a group	WEDGY	resembling a wedge
		WEEDY	resembling a weed
UGLY	displeasing to the sight	WEENY	tiny
UNARY	consisting of a single element	WEEPY	tending to weep
		WENNY	resembling a wen
UNDY	unde	WETLY	in a wet manner
UNIFY	make into a coherent whole	WHEY	watery part of milk
		WHINY	tending to whine
UNITY	the state of being one single entity	WHITY	whitey
		WHY	the reason or cause of something
UNLAY	to untwist		
UNSAY	retract something said	WIDDY	a hangman's noose
UPBY	upbye	WILLY	to willow
UPDRY	to dry completely	WILY	crafty
VARY	to become or make different	WINDY	marked by strong wind
		WINEY	winy
VASTY	vast	WINGY	swift

WINY	having the taste or qualities of wine
WIRY	resembling wire
WISPY	resembling a wisp
WITHY	a flexible twig
WITTY	humorously clever
WOMBY	hollow
WONKY	unsteady
WOODY	containing or resembling wood
WOOLY	woolly
WOOZY	dazed
WORDY	using many or too many words
WORRY	to feel anxious or uneasy
WRY	contorted
YAY	to this extent
YEUKY	itchy
YOLKY	resembling a yolk
YUMMY	delicious
ZANY	ludicrously comical
ZESTY	marked by zest
ZINCY	zincky
ZINGY	enjoyably exciting
ZINKY	zincky
ZIPPY	full of energy
ZLOTY	a monetary unit of Poland

Z - END

ABUZZ	buzzing	
ADZ	a cutting tool	
BLITZ	a sudden attack	
BORTZ	bort	
BUZZ	a vibrating sound	
CHEZ	at the home of	
COZ	a cousin	
FEZ	a brimless cap worn by men in the Near East	
FIZ	a hissing sound	
FIZZ	a hissing sound	
FRIZ	a tight curl	
FRIZZ	form into small tight curls	
FUZZ	to become fuzzy	
GROSZ	a Polish coin	
HAFIZ	a Muslim who knows the Koran by heart	
HERTZ	a unit of frequency	
JAZZ	to enliven	
JEEZ	used as a mild oath	
KLUTZ	a clumsy person	
NERTZ	nerts	
OYEZ	cry used to introduce the opening of a court of law	
PHIZ	a facial expression	
QUIZ	test knowledge by asking questions	
RAZZ	to deride	
RITZ	pretentious display	
SPITZ	dog having a heavy coat	
TOPAZ	a mineral	
TROOZ	trews	
WALTZ	a ballroom dance	
WHIZ	a buzzing sound	
WHIZZ	to whiz	
WIZ	very skillful person	

BIZ

Z - ALL

ABUZZ	buzzing
ADOZE	dozing
ADZ	a cutting tool
ADZE	adz
AGAZE	gazing
AMAZE	to overwhelm with surprise or wonder
AZAN	a Muslim call to prayer
AZIDE	a chemical compound
AZIDO	a chemical compound
AZO	containing nitrogen
AZOIC	geologic period before appearance of life
AZOLE	a chemical compound
AZON	radio-controlled aerial bomb
AZOTE	nitrogen
AZOTH	mercury
AZURE	a blue color
BAIZA	a monetary unit of Oman
BAIZE	green, woolen fabric
BAZAR	bazaar
BEZEL	a slanted surface
BEZIL	bezel
BIZE	bise
BLAZE	to bum brightly
BLITZ	a sudden attack
BONZE	a Buddhist monk
BOOZE	liquor
BOOZY	drunken
BORTZ	bort
BOZO	a fellow
BRAZA	a Spanish unit of length
BRAZE	to solder together
BUZZ	a vibrating sound
CHEZ	at the home of
CLOZE	type of reading comprehension test

COLZA	a type from cabbage
COZ	a cousin
COZEN	to deceive
COZEY	cozy
COZIE	cozy
COZY	snug and comfortable
CRAZE	to make insane
CRAZY	insane
CROZE	tool used in barrel-making
CZAR	an emperor or king
DAZE	to stun
DIAZO	containing a certain chemical group
DITZY	a twitter
DIZEN	to dress in fine clothes
DIZZY	having a sensation of whirling
DOOZY	doozer
DOZE	to sleep lightly
DOZEN	to stun
DOZER	one that dozes
DOZY	drowsy
ENYZM	enzyme
FAZE	to disturb the composure of
FEAZE	to faze
FEEZE	to faze
FEZ	brimless cap worn in the Near East
FIZ	a hissing sound
FIZZ	a hissing sound
FIZZY	a hissing sound
FOZY	too ripe
FRIZ	a tight curl
FRIZZ	form into small tight curls
FROZE	past tense of freeze
FURZE	a spiny shrub
FURZY	abounding in gorse

FUZE	to fuze	LAZY	disinclined to work
FUZEE	fusee	LEZZY	female that likes females
FUZIL	fusil	MAIZE	an American cereal grass
FUZZ	to become fuzzy	MATZA	matzo
FUZZY	blurry	MATZO	an unleavened bread
GAUZE	a transparent fabric	MAZE	to bewilder
GAUZY	resembling gauze	MAZER	a large drinking bowl
GAZE	to look intently	MAZY	full of confusing turns
GAZER	one that gazes	MEZZO	female voice of a full deep
GHAZI	a Muslim war hero		quality
GINZO	derogatory slur of a Sicilian	MIRZA	a Persian title of honor
GIZMO	gismo	MIZEN	mizzen
GLAZE	to fit windows with glass	MOZO	a manual laborer
	panes	MUZZY	confused
GLAZY	covered with a smooth,	NAZI	a type of fascist
	glossy coating	NERTZ	nerts
GLITZ	ostentatious showiness	NIZAM	a former sovereign of India
GLOZE	to explain away	NUDZH	an irritating person
GONZO	style of journalism	OOZE	to flow or leak out slowly
GRAZE	to feed on growing grass	OOZY	containing or resembling
GROSZ	a Polish coin		soft mud or slime
HAFIZ	Muslim who knows the	ORZO	rice shaped pasta
	Koran by heart	OUZEL	a European bird
HAMZA	Arabic diacritical mark	OUZO	a Greek liqueur
HAZAN	a cantor	OYEZ	cry used to introduce the
HAZE	subject to a humiliating		opening of a court of law
	initiation	OZONE	a form of oxygen
HAZEL	a shrub	PHIZ	a facial expression
HAZER	one that hazes	PIZZA	an Italian open pie
HAZY	unclear	PLAZA	a public square
HEEZE	to hoist	PRIZE	to value highly
HERTZ	a unit of frequency	QUIZ	test knowledge by asking
HUZZA	to cheer		questions
IZAR	an outer garment worn by	RAZE	tear down or demolish
	Muslim women	RAZEE	make lower by removing
JAZZ	to enliven		the upper deck as a ship
JAZZY	lively	RAZER	one that razes
JEEZ	used as a mild oath	RAZOR	sharp edged instrument
KAZOO	a toy musical instrument	RAZZ	to deride
KLUTZ	a clumsy person	RITZ	pretentious display
KUDZU	an Asian vine	RITZY	elegant
LAZAR	beggar afflicted with a	SEIZE	take hold suddenly and
	loathsome disease		forcibly
LAZE	to pass time lazily		

152

SIZAR	student who receives financial assistance	ZEIN	a simple protein
SIZE	physical proportions	ZERK	a grease fitting
SIZER	sizar	ZERO	the exact center of a target
SIZY	viscid	ZEST	invigorating excitement
SMAZE	atmospheric mixture of smoke and haze	ZESTY	marked by zest
SOZIN	a type of protein	ZETA	a Greek letter
SPITZ	dog having a heavy coat	ZIBET	an Asian civet
TAZZA	an ornamental bowl	ZIG	to turn sharply
TIZZY	state of nervous confusion	ZILCH	nothing
TOPAZ	a mineral	ZINC	a metallic element
TROOZ	trews	ZINCY	zincky
TZAR	czar	ZING	a high-pitched humming sound
UNZIP	to open the zipper of	ZINGY	enjoyably exciting
VIZIR	vizier	ZINKY	zincky
VIZOR	to visor	ZIP	move with speed and vigor
WALTZ	a ballroom dance	ZIPPY	full of energy
WAZOO	anus	ZIRAM	a chemical salt
WHIZ	a buzzing sound	ZITI	a tubular pasta
WHIZZ	to whiz	ZIZIT	fringes of the tallit
WINZE	steeply inclined mine shaft	ZLOTY	a monetary unit of Poland
WIZ	a very skillful person	ZOA	of zoon
WIZEN	to shrivel	ZOEA	larval form of certain crustaceans
WOOZY	dazed	ZOIC	pertaining to animals or animal life
ZAG	to turn sharply		
ZAIRE	a monetary unit of Zaire	ZOMBI	snake god voodoo cult
ZAMIA	a tropical plant	ZONAL	pertaining to a zone
ZANY	ludicrously comical	ZONE	areas distinguished from other adjacent areas
ZANZA	an African musical instrument	ZOO	place where animals are kept for exhibition
ZAP	to kill or destroy		
ZARF	a metal holder for a coffee cup	ZOOID	organic body capable of independent movement
ZAX	a tool for cutting roof slates	ZOOKS	used as a mild oath
		ZOOM	to move with a loud humming sound
ZAYIN	a Hebrew letter		
ZEAL	enthusiastic devotion	ZOON	the whole product of one fertilized egg
ZEBEC	xebec		
ZEBRA	African mammal that is related to the horse	ZORI	a type of sandal
		ZORIL	a small African mammal
ZEBU	an Asian ox	ZOUK	style of music
ZED	the letter Z	ZOWIE	used to express surprise or pleasure
ZEE	the letter Z		

ZUZ   a Jewish coin
ZYME   an enzyme

2 LETTER

AA	rough, cindery lava		HI	used as a greeting
AD	an advertisement		HO	used to express surprise
AE	one		ID	part of the psyche
AH	used to express delight or relief		IF	a possibility
AI	a three-toed sloth		IN	to harvest
AM	1st person sing of be		IS	present 3rd person singular of be
AN	used before words beginning with vowel		IT	3d person sing neuter pronoun
AR	the letter R		JO	a sweetheart
AS	to the same degree		KA	spiritual self of a human in Egyptian religion
AT	in position of		KI	plant native to Pacific islands and China
AW	used to express protest or disbelief		LA	the sixth tone of the diatonic musical scale
AX	type of cutting tool		LI	Chinese unit of distance
AY	aye		LO	used to attract attention or to express surprise
BA	the eternal soul in Egyptian mythology		MA	mother
BE	to exist		ME	I
BI	a bisexual		MI	third tone of the diatonic musical scale
BO	a pal		MU	a Greek letter
DA	used in names		MY	form of the pronoun I
DE	used in names and phrases		NO	a negative reply
DO	to begin and carry through to completion		NU	a Greek letter
EF	the letter F		OD	a hypothetical force of natural power
EH	used to express doubt or surprise		OF	used to indicate derivation from
EL	an elevated railroad		OH	to exclaim in surprise pain or desire
EM	the letter M		OK	
EN	the letter N		OM	mantra to contemplate ultimate reality
ER	used to express hesitation		ON	side of wicket batsman stands in cricket
ES	ess		OP	style of abstract art
ET	a past tense of eat		OR	grammatical conjunction
EX	the letter X		OS	an orifice or bone
FA	the fourth tone of the diatonic musical scale			
GO	to move along			
HA	a sound of surprise			
HE	a male person			

OW	used to express sudden pain
OX	a hoofed mammal
OY	exclamation of dismay
PA	a father
PE	a Hebrew letter
PI	mathematical constant
QI	animating force behind all forms of life
RE	the second tone of the diatonic musical scale
SH	used to urge silence
SO	sol
TA	an expression of gratitude
TI	the seventh tone of the diatonic musical scale
TO	in the direction of
UH	used to express hesitation
UM	used to fill a pause while speaking
UP	to raise
US	we
UT	musical tone in the French solmization system, now do
WE	1st person plural pronoun
WO	woe
XI	letter in Greek alphabet
XU	a monetary unit of Vietnam
YA	you
YE	yes
YO	used to greet someone

REFERENCES

The Editor is responsible for any errors in spelling or inaccuracies in definition. Words may have additional meanings. Some words may not be acceptable for tournaments or competitive events. New words are created all the time and we welcome suggestions for words for the next edition.

The American Heritage Dictionary, Second College Edition, Houghton Mifflin Company, 1982

The Official Scrabble Players Dictionary, Pocket Books, 1979

http://dictionary.reference.com

http://en.wikipedia.org

http://www.merriam-webster.com

http://www.thefreedictionary.com

http://www.urbandictionary.com

NOTES

NOTES

NOTES